HISTORIC ANCHORAGE

An Illustrated History

by John Strohmeyer

Published by the Anchorage Museum Association

Historical Publishing Network
A division of Lammert Publications, Inc.
San Antonio, Texas

ISBN: 1-893619-21-4

Library of Congress Card Catalog Number: 2001091146

Historic Anchorage: An Illustrated History

author:	John Strohmeyer
photo editor:	Hal Gage
contributing writer for "sharing the heritage":	Julie Johnson
museum archivist:	Diane Brenner

Historical Publishing Network

president:	Ron Lammert
vice president:	Barry Black
project representatives:	Joe Neely
	Robin Neely
director of operations:	Charles A. Newton, III
administration:	Angela Lake
	Donna M. Mata
	Dee Steidle
graphic production:	Colin Hart
	John Barr

PRINTED IN SINGAPORE

The air travel industry was born on the Anchorage Park Strip.

COURTESY OF THE ANCHORAGE MUSEUM OF HISTORY AND ART (B65.2.16).

CONTENTS

✧

Jack and Nellie Brown, the first residents of Ship Creek, built this fourteen-by-fourteen-foot forest tent in June 1912.
COURTESY OF THE ANCHORAGE MUSEUM OF HISTORY AND ART (B88.11.8).

CHAPTER I

3

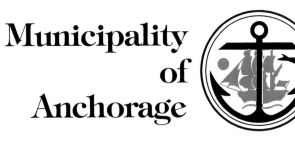

Municipality of Anchorage

P.O. Box 196650
Anchorage, Alaska 99519-6650
Telephone: (907) 343-4431
Fax: (907) 343-4499
http://www.ci.anchorage.ak.us

George P. Wuerch, Mayor

OFFICE OF THE MAYOR

HISTORIC ANCHORAGE, published by the Anchorage Museum Association, is a wonderful book about Alaska and our city of Anchorage.

Alaska, the Great State, provides the spiritual, economic, and cultural framework for our city. The state provides the bounds where dreams, ideas, and breath of thoughts can flourish. And flourish it has in our city. To understand the pioneer spirit we must relate to our boundless environment. To accept and understand Alaska, we must understand the goals and dreams of the pioneers of Anchorage.

HISTORIC ANCHORAGE speaks to our city and of the pioneers and individuals who helped its growth from its beginnings in 1915 to today. In fact, my grandfather worked on the Alaska railroad in the early part of the twentieth century. So I, like many others, retain a highly prized thread connecting the history of our forefathers in Alaska to the present day. This book is of particular interest because of the excellent text by John Strohmeyer, former Atwood Professor of Journalism at the University of Alaska, and because of the wonderful photographs from the collections of the Anchorage Museum of History and Art.

I enjoyed reading about the many businesses in our town whose histories are included in the book since their stories are central to understanding the thriving city that Anchorage is today.

Visitors are surprised to learn how young our city is. From its beginning as a tent city at the mouth of Ship Creek eighty-six years ago, Anchorage has grown to become the largest city in Alaska, with a population of more than 260,000. It is culturally diverse city, where people of many nationalities have come to seek their dreams amid our towering mountains and clean waters.

Anchorage is the economic center of the state and is located at the hub of the world's largest economy. Today, few U.S. cities can match the combination of cultural opportunities and outdoor activities that Anchorage residents enjoy within the city limits.

More than two hundred thousand visitors each year enjoy our Museum and learn about the history, art and cultures of Alaska through the Museum's varied exhibitions and public programs. I am particularly proud of the Anchorage Museum Association, the nonprofit support arm of the Anchorage Museum of History and Art, for its efforts in producing this book.

HISTORIC ANCHORAGE speaks for our past and our present. I hope that readers will be guided by the history they learn here and will be inspired to think about the exciting prospects that lie ahead for Anchorage of the future.

Happy reading!

George Weurch
Mayor of Anchorage

CHAPTER I

It would be hard to find any American city that has undergone more tumultuous changes in character and growth during the last century than Anchorage, the largest metropolis in Alaska. Gold exploration, railroad boom and bust, military occupation, air age discovery, oil fever, earthquakes, and finally massive oil wealth all figured into transforming this relatively recent wilderness site into a jewel of a city. How it happened is a great success story of American urbanization in unseemly places.

Anthropologists believe that a land bridge around twenty-five thousand years ago connected the continents of Asia and North America, and many contend that this brought the first waves of humans into what today is Alaska. However, none of those early inhabitants apparently headed for the Upper Cook Inlet, where Anchorage is located. Dr. William Workman, anthropology professor at the University of Alaska Anchorage, says human habitation of this region could not have occurred until fifteen thousand years ago at the earliest. That is when Wisconsin Ice, the latest glacier that shaped the mountains and carved out the inlet, is believed to have made its significant retreat.

Dr. Workman says clues found in excavations indicate that at least five different cultural traditions of perhaps 400 to 500 people each came and departed the upper Cook Inlet three thousand years years ago. None left clear evidence of continuity. "Why they left this resource-rich region remains a mystery," Workman says. "Maybe it was due to bad luck, wars, or bad weather but it seems as though they felt it was a good place to visit but not a good place to stay."

Not until 1778, when English explorer Captain James Cook sailed into the Cook Inlet on his third voyage in search of a Northwest passage, does history record some descriptions of the early residents of what is today Anchorage.

✧

An early settler feeds an orphan bear cub while his wary dog looks on.
COURTESY OF THE ANCHORAGE MUSEUM OF HISTORY AND ART (B80-41-120).

A statue of English explorer Captain James Cook stands at Resolution Park overlooking the Cook Inlet where he met early residents of what was to become Anchorage.
PHOTO BY HAL GAGE © 2001.

With his ships *Resolution* and *Discovery* swinging at anchor in the bay, Cook describes the first meeting on May 30, 1778: "Six canoes came off the east shore. They remained a short distance from the ships, viewing them with a kind of silent surprise. At length, they took courage and came alongside to barter. The Indians brought furs, salmon and halibut which they exchanged for old clothes and trinkets."

Today, a huge statute of Captain Cook, supposedly looking towards the historic meeting place in the distance, stands in Resolution Park, a western point of the city's downtown where it meets the Cook Inlet. The canoe people have been described as Tanaina Indians (Dena'ina), a semi-nomadic tribe that roamed the coast trading with other tribes and with the early Russian fur hunters.

No statues stand in honor of the area's earliest known inhabitants. Smallpox epidemics in the mid- and late 1800s decimated the tribe, and today Tanaina

survivors are loosely known by the public as Athabaskans. However, some in villages such as Eklutna and Tyonek still try to preserve the Dena'ina culture.

In 1867 the United States purchased Alaska from Russia for $7.2 million, roughly two cents an acre. However, even with reports of rich resources in the new territory, no great rush developed to explore Alaska until miners Joe Juneau and Richard Harris discovered gold near the Gastineau Channel in 1880. With steam-powered vessels by now more reliable, Alaska became more accessible. Stampeders rushed in. The gold-seeking throngs eventually created the new town of Juneau almost overnight and soon provided it the population credentials to replace Sitka as the capital.

Then, within the next ten years, gold miners struck it rich in the Yukon, the Canadian territory bordering Alaska. Next, word spread that gold nuggets were washing up on the beaches in Norton Sound, and thus the city of Nome sprang forth. That population explosion of miners and suppliers created a bustling interior trading post, and Fairbanks was born.

Yet, Captain Cook had noted that this mountain-sheltered, ocean accessible plain at the head of the Cook Inlet was "as favorable a settlement as any under the same latitude." While gold explorers did stop nearby to mine claims at Hope and Willow Creek, virtually nothing was happening to future Anchorage during this invasion by outsiders.

Fortunately, its early potential was not altogether overlooked, though more by

✧

Timber pilings are laid in place to support Alaska Railroad track rounding Turnagain Arm.

CHAPTER I

accident than design. During the early 1900s, Wallace Atwood, a young Harvard instructor trained as a geologist and physiographer, spent several summers in Alaska compiling geological reports for the United States Geological Survey. One of the geological structures he studied was at the head of the Cook Inlet, the present townsite of Anchorage. His findings would have a profound impact later in a scenario he never would have imagined.

So neither gold, coal, timber, fish nor furs, the much publicized resources of the new territory, figured in the development of early Anchorage. In fact the city sprang from a colony of squatters, most of them desperately hunting for jobs on an anticipated railroad and living in tents, hastily thrown up as temporary homes.

In May 1915 the federal government began laying 470 miles of railroad track that would connect the ice-free port of Seward in the

south to the interior trading capital at Fairbanks. Only once before, in building a rail system to serve the Panama Canal, had the federal government financed building a railroad. The major public purpose of this venture was to access the massive coal fields in the Matanuska Valley to serve the Pacific fleet, which had to depend on coal hauled from eastern Pennsylvania, a distance from the west coast that is about halfway around the world.

The Alaskan Engineering Commission, the federal agency designated to build the railroad, selected Anchorage as its headquarters because it was about midway on the line and had a protected anchorage that could be dredged at Ship Creek. No sooner had the SS *Mariposa*, carrying Chief Construction Commissioner Lieutenant Frederick Mears and his advance staff, landed at Ship Creek in mid-May of 1915, when a vessel loaded with job-seeking people came virtually in its wake.

The hordes of newcomers, consisting mainly of homeless European immigrants who had emigrated to the West Coast but could not find work, pitched a city of tents along Ship Creek. The railroad eventually hired many of them as day laborers at $3 a day. However, the lack of toilets, accentuated by the pollution of drinking water, created such immense sanitation problems that the government had to defer its resources from railroad building to create a livable town instead.

The AEC tried to move the squatters up to the Eklutna River, about twenty-eight miles to the north. The squatters resisted, and about this time the *Cook Inlet Pioneer*, a crude but readable newspaper, appeared on the scene. It quickly took up their cause. When Alaska's delegate to congress, James Wickersham, prodded federal bureaucrats to support the squatters, the commission yielded and hastily assigned railroad engineers to lay out a town.

An aerial view of Anchorage, c. 1930.
COURTESY OF THE ANCHORAGE MUSEUM OF
HISTORY AND ART (B82.1.33.27).

They platted a 350-acre, rectangular townsite on a plateau overlooking Ship Creek. Seeking the simplest (and fastest) method to create a town, they numbered the east-west running streets and named the north-south running streets with letters, omitting "J" street, reportedly, the story goes, as a courtesy to the Scandinavians who had trouble pronouncing the letter.

On July 10, 1915, the government sold lots, now partially cleared of trees, at an auction.

General Land Office Sales Representative Andrew Christensen, served as auctioneer. In the two-day sale, 655 lots were sold at an aggregate of $148,000. Prices ranged from a high of $1,150 for a most desirable commercial location to $25 for the lowest appraised home sites. L. F. Shaw, founder and editor of the *Cook Inlet Pioneer*, ecstatically devoted the front page of his July 17 issue proclaiming that the sale was a huge success. Though still unnamed, the town of Anchorage was born.

CHAPTER II

The boom from railroad building that occurred in Anchorage is reminiscent of the gold rushes that preceded in other parts of Alaska. As the settlers chopped down trees and burned stumps, filling the air with smoke and dust, log cabins and tents sprouted. And within a month, so did commercial enterprises.

The Pioneer Hotel, F. B. Cannon, Prop., offered accommodations for ninety guests (no bar but a private lobby for ladies). Browns and Hawkins, general merchandise, featured "Native Lumber, Rough and Dressed, of All Dimensions." Anchorage Central Market advertised fresh meats ranging from "No. 1 Steer Beef" to "Pigs Feet, etc."

Captain Austin Lathrop, one of Alaska's earliest resident millionaires, compounded his successes in Cordova and Fairbanks by erecting the most commodious building in the new town. He bought the corner of Fourth Avenue and H Street (roughly the site of today's famed Fourth Avenue Theater) and leased out five store spaces. "The door is the best ever placed in an Alaska building," the *Cook Inlet Pioneer* said in lauding Lathrop's edifice.

Carroll & Co. added what might have been the first esthetic touches to downtown. It installed plate glass on the entire fifty-foot frontage of its store building and leased part of it to Sydney Laurence, Alaska's famed artist, for his photograph gallery.

Two banks, including a branch that was to become headquarters for the National Bank of Alaska, erected instant offices to fuel the boom. The Montana Pool Room was among the first to accommodate the population's sporting instincts. And just outside the townsite boundaries, a district was set up for prostitutes to cater to the less eclectic. (The railroad commission barred liquor sales and gambling dens but chose not to interfere with the world's oldest profession. In fact, it provided land for a red-light district free of charge.)

From the time the first railroad construction crews arrived, the *Cook Inlet Pioneer* urged that the town incorporate and get out from under the yoke of the federal government. In May 1916, it even changed

✧

Young men being recruited to serve in the army in World War I, c. 1918.

COURTESY OF THE ANCHORAGE MUSEUM OF HISTORY AND ART (BL79.2.4971).

the name of its paper to the *Anchorage Daily Times*, "in order to keep the town of Anchorage more prominently before the reading public." When the Anchorage Chamber of Commerce was founded that same month, it joined the campaign to put Anchorage on the map.

As the railroad's mid-point commissioner for the three-member Alaskan Engineering Commission, Frederick Mears was sympathetic to civic needs. He used AEC funds to build a schoolhouse during the town's first year. He provided a commissary for employees, built a two-story log hospital, and staffed a mess hall where workers could eat for thirty-three cents a meal.

Mears even asked the *Cook Inlet Pioneer* to conduct a contest to choose a name for the still nameless settlement. In the first school board election on August 2, 1915, voters also got a

chance to vote on a choice of nine names. Folklore, now embedded in many Anchorage histories, tells us Anchorage won handily, apparently since most people felt it was the port which influenced the railroad to establish its headquarters here. Not so, according to records of the Alaskan Engineering Commission dug up by M. Diane Brenner, archivist for the Anchorage Museum of History and Art.

The document shows that the top vote getter was Alaska City at 146 votes. Second in the voting was Lane (in honor of the then-secretary of interior), with 129. Anchorage came in third, with 101 ballots, about nineteen percent of the total votes cast. Then came Matanuska, which had great visibility because of its identity with the nearby coal fields. The other names on the ballot were Gateway, Ship Creek, Homestead, Terminal, and Winalaska.

It appears that the U.S. Post Office arbitrarily had named the new settlement Anchorage. The Chamber of Commerce tried to change the name to Alaska City to be consistent with the vote. Alaskan Engineering Commissioner Mears so notified his chairman, W. C. Edes, in Seward, who telegraphed the request to Andrew Christensen, chief of the Alaska Field Division, General Land Office, then operating out of Seattle. A flurry of telegrams ensued until the matter was laid to rest by a letter dated October 1915 from Mears to Edes suggesting that no immediate action be taken on the Chamber of Commerce request.

He indicated local businessmen were having second thoughts, and Secretary of Interior Lane had responded and felt it was best to leave the matter alone "for the present." Despite the vote, Anchorage got its name from the whim of some anonymous postal worker.

With the ending of World War I, Congress engaged in fierce debates over further appropriations as money continued to run out for the still unfinished railroad. In 1920 it applied a drastic cost-cutting measure. Mears was notified that the AEC would henceforth be relieved of any responsibility for the town. That virtually forced the incorporation issue. In an election held on November 23, 1920, Anchorage voters duly incorporated the city.

The first council meeting of the newly-formed City of Anchorage was held on November 26, 1920, at a place known as the Townsite Office, the dust-covered federal building. The lack of street lighting, the problems of illicit liquor traffic and free roaming dogs and cattle occupied the early attention of that first council.

Leopold David, a U.S. commissioner, the highest vote-getter in that first election, was seated as mayor. Others elected to council were Frank I. Reed, owner of the Anchorage Hotel; John J. Longacre, chief electrician for the railroad; Isador Bayles, men's clothing store owner; D. H. Williams, undertaker; A. C. Craig, carpenter foreman on the railroad; and Ralph W. Moyer, manager of the Bank of Alaska, one of two banks already doing business.

On January 21, 1921, council passed the first budget, a proposed expenditure of approximately $12,000 based on a six-mill property tax levy. Estimates placed the valuation of real and personal property in Anchorage at $2,192,450, although numerous protests and appeals later would significantly lower that expectation.

Minutes of the next meetings show that council voted unanimously to erect fifteen street lights. It decided to license dogs but split on the removal of curtains in poolrooms, cigar stores and other public places where people congregate to gamble. But council members vigorously agreed on the need for the early appointment of a police chief to keep the gamblers and other lawbreakers in check.

Sixty-year-old John J. Sturgus, a former federal agent, won the job as the town's first police chief. On February 16, 1921, sitting at his first council meeting, the new chief listened with others as an irate person complained about crime, which is recorded in the minutes as follows:

"A prominent citizen and family man appeared before council and issued an oral complaint that a number of immoral houses are in existence in the vicinity of between 6th and 9th Streets on C Street. They are multiplying and encroaching on such streets as 7th and 8th. Men appear in all hours of the night…they are noisy and troublesome…children have to pass these immoral houses on the way to school."

✧

Top: The Yukon Room, a tent bunkhouse, being moved on skids to a location on Fourth Avenue in downtown Anchorage.
COURTESY OF THE ANCHORAGE MUSEUM OF HISTORY AND ART (B79.1.78).

Above: A striking view from Government Hill shows the sun cycle over a tent city during the winter solstice in 1917.
COURTESY OF THE ANCHORAGE MUSEUM OF HISTORY AND ART (B94.2.85).

It was clear that purveyors of prostitution were crossing their established boundary. Council told Chief Sturgus to "enforce the law." However, four days later, Sturgus was shot to death. His body was found lying in a snow bank at the rear of Anchorage Drug Store near Fourth Avenue. Despite a $2,000 reward, neither the motive nor identity of his killer was determined. The *Anchorage Daily Times*, now owned by ex-miner Charley Herron, showed it had lost none of its editorial zest. It strongly blamed the murder on an "illicit liquor gang" which, it said, was running the town.

It seemed that the gang also meant to send a message to future police chiefs. Sturgus' successor resigned after a few months on the job, apparently realizing that he, too, was a marked man. He was followed by Harry Kavanaugh, also a former federal agent. Chief Kavanaugh was murdered on January 2, 1924, the second Anchorage police chief killed in less than three years.

Kavanaugh was shot down by what the *Anchorage Times* described as a "drunken Bad Indian," who had been on the lam from a double murder. Once more, the *Times* took the occasion to deplore the death, editorially blaming the "illegal liquor traffickers," the aforementioned scourge of the town.

After such a start, it is hard to envision how anything good could come out of this unruly frontier settlement. And for many years thereafter not much did. In 1923 President Harding came up to drive the traditional golden spike. The railroad was finally finished. And so were the thousand or so jobs of the people who built it. Further, the Navy by now had converted to oil for fuel. It no longer needed the Matanuska coal and that eliminated even more jobs.

While Congress stopped short of abandoning the project, heeding pleas it would devastate the little communities on the rail belt, it appropriated only enough funds to cover the operating deficit. That was small comfort. Unemployed laborers withdrew their savings accounts from the banks and left town to search for jobs elsewhere.

"The overexpansion of business in Anchorage during the railroad boom of the early 1920s brought on the inevitable bust of the mid-1920s," the National Bank of Alaska says in assessing its branch's losses in its blockbuster history published in 2000. "Old-timers had seen the depressing cycle strike many times before. Whenever business had been too good for too long, it seems the same old story," Bank President Edward A. Rasmuson said. "A town runs up in a hurry and gradually goes down until there is very little left except worry for those who are in business."

Now it remained to be seen whether infant Anchorage, born out of the railroad boom, could survive the bust.

CHAPTER III

By 1923 Anchorage, indeed, was left with very little—one railroad track, no road system and no decent payroll to support it. One northbound train a week chugged into the station bringing passengers and mail from the weekly steamship that came from Seattle and unloaded in Seward. The train would go on to Fairbanks, turn around, and come back through Anchorage and on to Seward to meet the next weekly steamer.

With coal no longer important to Washington, hopes were that the railroad could survive by the development of mines and other new business along the rail belt. These failed to materialize, and the railroad losses mounted. Congress grew increasingly skeptical on whether to keep the railroad running.

In an interview with the *New York Times* in 1926, Representative Allen T. Treadway of Massachusetts explained why he opposed any more public money for "worthless Alaska." "Experience is sometimes an expensive teacher and this is true of this country's expenditure in a country where the thermometer itself freezes and where darkness obtains six months each year. Americans never can be persuaded to migrate there unless supernatural power changes nature itself."

✧

Pioneer civic leader Robert S. Bragaw, for whom a street in Anchorage is named, is fourth from the left on the front row in this photo of Anchorage's earliest leading citizens.

COURTESY OF THE ANCHORAGE MUSEUM OF HISTORY AND ART (B00.3).

And they felt in their bones that something good would come to save their city. Their dogged commitment to the potential of Anchorage matches the blind confidence of those settlers who won the West.

The backgrounds of those brave—some say foolhardy—merchant pioneers are as diverse as the land itself. One was Zachary J. Loussac, born in Russia in 1882. At the age of eighteen, he immigrated to New York and enrolled at the New York School of Pharmacy. With degree in hand, he headed west to seek his fortune. He stopped at Seattle but soon headed north to Haines, gateway to the Yukon gold strikes, and started a drug store. As that gold rush fizzled, he moved to Juneau, where gold fever still prevailed. However, he stayed only briefly when he heard that a new town was being formed by the Alaska Railroad in Anchorage.

Loussac arrived in Anchorage in 1916. He opened a drug store on Fourth Avenue and soon did well enough to open a second, which also sold newspapers and books. His development instincts led him to become one of the founders of the Evan Jones Coal Mining Co. in the Matanuska coal fields.

The enterprising Loussac managed to ride out the lean years even though profits were virtually nil. But when gathering war clouds forced the military to build defenses in Alaska in the early 1940s, he was positioned to take advantage of the population influx. He sold his drug stores and interest in the coal mine and teamed up with Dr. Harold Sogn, one of the few resident physicians in Anchorage, to build the largest office building in Anchorage.

The Loussac-Sogn Building on Fifth Avenue and D Street housed Dr. Sogn's clinic among other well-heeled renters. It was valued at more than a half a million dollars. The income made Loussac a rich man, but unlike some others who came up to exploit the boom, he didn't pocket his windfall and run. Instead, he created the Loussac Foundation to provide grants to charitable organizations.

In 1947 Loussac was elected mayor of the City of Anchorage. After leaving office, his foundation assumed the obligation to pay off $350,000 in bonds so the city could build a public library. When it opened in

With the massive layoffs by the railroad and support shops, most of Anchorage's original adventurers lit out for other places, many leaving unpaid loans and mortgages behind them. But a few of the town's leaders decided to try to ride out the bust. They catered to the skeleton work force that remained in Anchorage to run the railroad.

1955, the city dedicated it as the Z. J. Loussac Public Library.

The new handsome structure, totally wired into the nation's inter-library network, is a stunning sight on Thirty-sixth Avenue in midtown. Besides serving as the center of the city's library system, the building is used today for many cultural and educational events, as well as meeting headquarters for the Anchorage Assembly. It is a permanent

tribute to Loussac, the Russian-born entrepreneur, who is generally regarded as the first philanthropist in Anchorage.

Jacob Gottstein, another original Anchorage merchant, came in 1915. Born in Iowa in 1886, he headed west at an early age and mastered pioneer grocery merchandising the hard way. In winter, he would walk into towns along the Fraser River in Canada taking orders. When ice went out, he shipped in the groceries on river boats. When the Canadian Railroad was built in the early 1900s, he visited the little mining towns along the route and also found eager customers.

By the age of twenty-seven, Gottstein had saved $25,000 and took off—to see the exotic cities of Europe. He quickly blew his poke. Returning after a year, he headed for Anchorage as soon as he heard that the government planned to build a railroad. He arrived with a case of cigars, bought a tent, and spent his first winter in a tent. He opened the J. B. Gottstein Wholesale Grocery Co. and started repeating his Fraser River routine.

Using dogsled and snowshoes in the winter, Gottstein visited camps sprouting up along the railroad construction. It took him five days to reach Seward, but he established faithful customers along the route.

Opposite, top: Anchorage Mayor Zachary J. Loussac, the father of philanthropy in Anchorage, also promoted Alaskan products at the Seattle Sports and Vacation Show.
COURTESY OF THE ANCHORAGE MUSEUM OF HISTORY AND ART (B75.134.151).

Opposite, bottom: The Z. J. Loussac Public Library was dedicated on June 1, 1955, in what the Anchorage Daily News *hailed as "a significant milestone in the modern development of Alaska."*
COURTESY OF THE ANCHORAGE MUSEUM OF HISTORY AND ART (B62.X.11.6).

Above: Jacob B. "Jake" Gottstein arrived in the new railroad town of Anchorage carrying a case of cigars and launched a wholesale grocery business.
COURTESY OF THE ANCHORAGE MUSEUM OF HISTORY AND ART (B00.3).

Below: Bernard J. "Barney" Gottstein built upon his father's legacy and teamed with Larry Carr to build a real estate and supermarket empire.
COURTESY OF THE ANCHORAGE MUSEUM OF HISTORY AND ART (B00.3).

As a provider of the basics, Gottstein managed to weather the lean times after the railroad crews left. He still had a flourishing business when in 1950 a heart attack forced him to turn over management of his grocery business to his son, Bernard, known as Barney.

With that father-son changeover, the Gottstein impact on Anchorage was to become even greater. Barney had done a stint in the U.S. Army Air Corps and came home with a college degree from the University of Washington. While learning grocery whole-saling, Barney met Larry Carr, a retail clerk, who, like himself, was another young turk looking to Alaska for a future.

Carr had left his home in California in 1947 at the age of eighteen and headed for Anchorage. He found jobs in a commissary and drug store and got to know J. C. Morris, a real estate developer. Morris happened to have a grocery tenant going broke. Impressed with Carr's hustle, Morris gave Larry, then still a teenager, a chance to revive the store. Larry started buying from the Gottstein wholesale store and thus began one of Anchorage's most important business partnerships.

Both young men became well-versed in the latest innovations in grocery merchandising They saw a chance to give Anchorage something better than its staid mom-and-pop stores, many of them still mired in a frontier mentality. Barney had wholesale and logistics knowledge—and money. Larry and his wife, Wilma (Moseley), knew the modern retailing touches lacking in Alaska.

The Carr-Gottstein partnership started in 1957 when the two entrepreneurs took over a struggling store in Fairbanks. Two years later they built the first combination unit in Alaska, wherein, besides groceries, the store sold drugs and a little of everything else. The development of the Carr's Food Center and the Carr-Gottstein real estate empire from their headquarters in Anchorage is a proud Alaska saga. By subsequently merging their wholesale and retail business, the pair raised the capital to launch the largest and most modern supermarket chain in the state and captured some of the primest real estate locations in Anchorage.

Tourists today are still awed by the sophisticated products in the eighteen Carr's and Eagle supermarkets in Anchorage.

Besides all the basics, shoppers can find five kinds of mushrooms, all varieties of fresh salad greens, from head lettuce to mesculin, and other items carried only by the fanciest metropolitan markets in the lower forty-eight.

In 1998 the Carr-Gottstein food store business, which started with a single, struggling store in the 1950s, was sold to Safeway for $330 million. Meanwhile, giant chains such as Fred Meyer have moved in to compete. By all appearances, Anchorage can claim that their shopping marts are as modern as any in the United States.

Anchorage reaped another dividend from this success story. The philanthropy of Larry Carr and Barney Gottstein also made Anchorage a better city. Among their deeds, they helped Alaska Pacific University when it was in critical financial need. In fact, Larry

Carr became chairman of the university's board of trustees at the time of the crisis.

Visitors to Anchorage are likely to encounter the impact of several other early Anchorage settlers who made lifelong commitments and are now enshrined in history.

Arnold Muldoon, a carpenter raised in Lancaster, Wisconsin, came to Anchorage in the doldrums of the 1930s and homesteaded what seemed to be regarded as a large wasteland east of Anchorage. It was then known as a boondocks where coyotes and wolves howled at night. He tried "proving" up his homestead by clearing several acres for oats, barley, clover, and timothy hay. But nothing grew. Muldoon conceded the area was not meant to be farmed because "there was practically no soil at all, just gravel and moss."

However, as a person who friends say enjoyed walking through his trees, Muldoon had the vision to recognize that his land might have even a greater use for Anchorage. He gave a large parcel to the city as public park land and later sold 74 acres more to the city at less than half of its appraised value. Today the public park preserves a swath of undeveloped land that runs four blocks wide.

The dirt path that once led to Muldoon's homestead cabin is now a major thoroughfare named Muldoon Road. Furthermore, the large commercial and residential district that the road spawned in East Anchorage appears on the city map as Muldoon.

Robert S. Bragaw came out of Idaho in 1918 to gamble on the growth of the new town of Anchorage. He set up a photography and gift shop but civic service soon became his main

TAMING EARLY ANCHORAGE

From the start, different elements in town tried to provide their own diversions outside of the job. Baseball was the town's favorite sport. It seemed everyone played, and even before the railroad was completed, the press reported the rivalry between Anchorage and Seward baseball teams as legendary.

For socializing and camaraderie they established chapters of the best proper fraternal lodges—the Elks, the Masons, the Moose, the Odd Fellows, and even the Eagles. And for the not so proper, sinister types provided gambling games that flourished day and night in the back rooms of the pool halls and cigar stores.

However, one important element for the full life was missing. If Anchorage was ever going to be transformed from a land of bachelors and bunkhouses to a land of families and bungalows, the town badly needed more women. So desperate was the need, that the Bridegroom Club was organized and its national appeal for brides made front page news in the *Daily Times*.

By 1922, Anchorage had a district court. The newsletter for the Pioneer Igloos of Alaska had some fun reporting the following early court incident:

"Pat, an old sourdough, was hustled into Joe Conroy's police court. It appears that Pat had called a lady a cow. After Conroy fined him $25 and costs, Pat addressed the court. 'Your honor,' he said, 'Is there any law against calling a cow a lady?'

'No,' replied Joe. 'I am not aware of any such statute.'

Pat turned to the offended female and with a bow of profound courtesy, he said: 'Good morning, lady.'

'Order in the courtroom!' thundered Judge Conroy."

occupation. He was the city clerk and treasurer of Anchorage, the first president of the Rotary Club, and secretary of the Anchorage Power & Light Co., the private enterprise that built the first hydroelectric plant at Eklutna. He served two terms in the early territorial Senate, a period when legislators received per diem, but no salary. And for many years he held the non-paying job of secretary of the Anchorage Chamber of Commerce. Bragaw Street, a bustling thoroughfare that links central Anchorage to the Glenn Highway, today memorializes his name.

Joe Spenard, a flamboyant character out of Canada, landed in Valdez about 1910. After failing to make a go with a store that sold everything from used mining equipment to secondhand clothing, he started a push cart business. When he came to Anchorage in 1916 to get in on the railroad boom, he replaced his pushcart with a bright, yellow REO truck and somehow found a yellow suit to match. He advertised his taxi business as the City Express, even though Anchorage had no roads leading anywhere.

While Spenard's express business leaves no legacy of notable history, his daunting style does. He homesteaded 160 acres bordering on what was then known as Jeter Lake in Chugach National Forest. There he promptly built a dance pavilion and carved out a swimming beach. The waterfront became a popular spot for the recreation-starved city, and people began calling it Spenard Lake.

It didn't seem to matter to Spenard that his budding resort was in a national forest

At last a paved street appeared in Anchorage in 1939. Rutted Fourth Avenue benefited from New Deal subsidies. A twenty-one-foot-wide concrete street with seventeen feet of asphalt edges was laid.
COURTESY OF THE ANCHORAGE MUSEUM OF HISTORY AND ART. (B00.23.7).

Joe Spenard's First car in Anchorage

and not open to homesteading, much less commercializing. But the dance pavilion burned down in 1917 before the feds could mount a court challenge. Soon after, Spenard left Alaska.

However, the dirt lane that Spenard opened to the lake became known as Spenard Road. Many seeking to avoid city taxes built homes along the road and enjoyed the services and schools of Anchorage without having to support the system. Mingled among them were gambling dens and bungalows where ladies of the night hung out shingles offering escort and massage services with names like Thee Body Shop, Alaskan Trapline, and Paradise Unlimited.

In 1949, some fifteen years after Joe Spenard's death and long after he moved to California, the area became the Spenard Public

Above: With typical flourish, Joe Spenard tools around the neighborhood in his insignia car.
COURTESY OF THE ANCHORAGE MUSEUM OF HISTORY AND ART (B99.15.5).

Below: Lake Spenard became a popular bathing beach resort even though Joe Spenard encroached upon national forest property.
COURTESY OF THE ANCHORAGE MUSEUM OF HISTORY AND ART (AEC.H.77).

LAKE SPENARD ANCHORAGES BATHING RESORT.

Utility District and was eventually annexed to
the city. While jokes about Spenard underlife are
common and suspect establishments still
prevail, a flourishing community known as
Spenard exists there today. National hotel chains
and restaurants moved in to take advantage of
the proximity to the Anchorage International
Airport. Two popular nightclubs—Chilkoot
Charlie's and the Fly by Night Club—help make
the area a fun place to visit.

CHAPTER IV

For twenty years after its founding, Anchorage remained part of an all-but-forgotten federal colony. Congress did not seem to know what to do with Alaska and seemed to care less. That left Anchorage dead in the water.

Without gold, fish, or minerals to provide income, the fate of Anchorage rested upon the whims of the federal government. The feds brought in the railroad, and, after it was built in 1923, the city largely lived off the meager income generated by being the railroad headquarters.

By 1935 even that tenuous lifeline was stressed. The railroad steadily raised rates, appeasing those clamoring in Congress to reduce deficits but hurting nearly every Alaskan because their livelihoods depended on goods shipped from out-of-state. Further, the monopolistic railroad used its clout to prevent any seaport development that might offer cheaper freight rates. Government subsidized the railroad's deficits, so nothing was permitted that might rob the railroad of business.

It was in the midst of this desolate period that fresh vigor was pumped into Anchorage life by the arrival of a new publisher of the all but bankrupt *Anchorage Daily Times*. Robert B. Atwood, a Clark University-educated journalist, and his civic-conscious bride, Evangeline, a former Chicago social worker, took over the paper in 1935.

✧

A family from the American Midwest arrives at Palmer Railroad Station on the way to a farm in the Matanuska Valley agricultural colony.

COURTESY OF THE ANCHORAGE MUSEUM OF HISTORY AND ART (B86.4.205).

Atwood was a young but astute reporter working on the Worcester, Massachusetts *Telegram* at the time, and Evangeline, who had a master's degree from the University of Chicago, was a well-connected partner, the daughter of E. A. Rasmuson, head of a major bank in town. Banker Rasmuson informed his son-in-law that the Anchorage paper had come on hard times and was available. Would Bob be interested in coming up to run it?

Atwood decided to consult with his geographer uncle, Wallace W. Atwood, who in 1911 did the scientific study of the Alaska peninsula for the U.S. Geological Survey. Wallace, now president of Clark University, told his nephew that Anchorage had all of the physical features needed for it to grow into an important American city. If it were up to him, Wallace said, he would go.

With his banker father-in-law underwriting the whole works, Atwood bought the sickly, 650-circulation *Anchorage Daily Times* for $10,000. The city had only twenty-two hundred people, barely more than it had when it was incorporated twenty years earlier. That Bob Atwood in the next forty years developed that paper into the largest daily in Alaska ranks among journalism's best success

stories. Further, this single publisher's impact on the development of Anchorage into the state's greatest city rivals the achievements of the most fabled American newspaper giants.

Atwood amazed many when, right off, he challenged the city's sacred cow—the virtually untouchable railroad. Atwood pointed out that Alaskans were paying more than five times as much as northwest states to haul basic foods. That set off a series of editorial fights with Colonel Otto Ohlson, the iron-fisted railroad boss, which became the talk of the town. Public pressures finally forced the colonel to temper the rate hikes and promise to look into the other complaints.

Then, during that same year of 1935, despite the constant threat to shut down the railroad over its budget problems, the city finally felt a slight relief from the federal axe hanging over its head. Under a "New Deal" project to help the indigent, the government announced it was sending Alaska 202 families from the farm-depressed states of Minnesota, Wisconsin and Michigan. They would settle in the nearby Matanuska Valley, to which Anchorage was linked by rail. The government would clear the land for planting and open a road to Anchorage. Each family was allotted forty acres and the promise of a house and barn.

While the Alaska Territorial Chamber of Commerce, headquartered in Juneau, and

THE CUDDY FAMILY

The First National Bank of Alaska, the second largest in Alaska, opened in Anchorage on January 30, 1922, despite protests from Alaska congressional delegate Dan Sutherland, among others, that this little railroad settlement could not support a new national bank.

It seems the critics were nearly right. Less than one month after the opening, crews laid the last steel rail connecting the south and north links. President Harding came up to drive in the golden spike signaling completion of the railroad. Workers were laid off in droves. The boom was over. Many pocketed their savings or withdrew their bank deposits and headed elsewhere to look for work.

How First National not only survived but grew into a formidable institution is one of the few success stories that can trace its beginning to that era. Essentially, it occurred because of the intelligent stewardship of one banking family.

With the help of some people associated with building the railroad, Winfield Ervin, a candy maker, founded the bank. He shared quarters with a furniture store, installed brass teller cages, made counters out of the marble slabs he had used to knead candy in Idaho, and equipped the room with polished brass spittoons. He managed to run the business with one employee, a railroad worker.

The influx of over a hundred farming families in the Matanuska Valley in 1935 might have been the most crucial development for the fortunes of the struggling bank. Not only did it provide new customers, but it brought a most important person into the bank's orbit. Warren Cuddy, one of the few prominent attorneys in Alaska, served on the board of directors of the Alaska Relief and Rehabilitation Corporation, which managed the corporation.

In 1941, Warren Cuddy bought controlling interest in the First National Bank. A former district attorney in Valdez, Warren became president of the bank and steered it on a path of growth, mainly by parlaying its national certification to win government business. His bank was chosen to supply the payroll for all the troops stationed in Alaska.

Still in the family, heirs of First National Bank pioneer Warren Cuddy are Betsy Lawler, vice chair and chief operating officer (left); son Dan H. Cuddy, chairman of the board (right); and Dan's wife, Betti Cuddy (center).

COURTESY OF CHRIS AREND.

When Warren Cuddy died in 1951, Cuddy's widow, Lucy Hon Cuddy, became chairman of the board, and their son, Dan, became the bank's new president. Dan, Stanford-educated and an attorney, led the bank through years of expansion. Its total assets topped $1 billion by 1989, and, by the end of the century, it had twenty-eight branches statewide.

A strong supporter of starting businesses, First National made sizable contributions to provide start up funding for the University of Alaska's small business development center.

In honor of Dan's mother, Lucy Hon Cuddy, once a university regent, the banking family spearheaded a $350,000 fund drive to modernize the culinary teaching program at the University of Alaska Anchorage. Besides providing the upscale Lucy Cuddy Dining Room, the support helps the culinary arts and hospitality center to teach the latest in cuisines. Instead of concentrating on teaching chefs for pipeline jobs, the emphasis is now changed to teaching the latest techniques to serve the state's burgeoning tourist businesses.

A third generation of Cuddys took over leadership of the bank in 1992. While Dan Cuddy remained as chairman, his daughter, Duke-educated Betsy Lawler, became vice chair and chief operating officer. In 1997 First National moved its corporate headquarters into a new high rise building at Thirty-sixth and A Street.

many legislators criticized the the idea of sending welfare families here, Anchorage cheered. Bob Atwood and Colonel Ohlson practically outdid one another in hailing the plan because it would send new people committed to stay. Even an avid Republican critic of the New Deal concept, E. A. Rasmuson, whose bank was reeling from several hard hits from the Depression, surprised his fellow Republican naysayers. He authorized his bank to make large additional loans to the struggling Eklutna power plant so it could serve the Matanuska Valley colony.

While the Matanuska project turned out to be a limited success in developing agriculture, it did open a wilderness adjoining Anchorage. It gave many downtrodden families a chance to live in dignity and rear children, many of whom became Alaska's current leaders. The influx of more people with diverse skills accelerated a transformation that would eventually make Anchorage Alaska's dominant city.

CHAPTER V

In the summer of 1939, two big amphibious military planes with the capacity to land anywhere put down on the grass strip of Merrill Field within the City of Anchorage. For the next several mornings the planes took off, circling the wilderness outside of town before heading elsewhere.

It didn't take Anchorage residents long to speculate that the federal government was finally recognizing the strategic importance of defending Alaska. Both Japan and Russia were building arsenals next door. It was widely assumed that the planes were on a reconnaissance mission to evaluate Anchorage as a military base.

But would help come in time? As late as 1940, the United States had a total of only two hundred troops stationed in Alaska, and they were based in the southeastern, landlocked port town of Haines. A twenty-year-old tugboat was their main means of transportation. With the enemy practically on its borders, Alaska needed a crash defense program, but after Congress had neglected Alaska for so many years, could it now understand the urgency?

Spirits in Anchorage were lifted in the spring of 1939 when President Roosevelt signed a land withdrawal order that designated fifty thousand acres adjacent to Anchorage for a military reservation. However, Alaska's delegate to Congress, Anthony Dimond, was frustrated when he tried to expedite a bill to appropriate $12,734,000 to build the first air base. It seemed Tampa in Florida, though well isolated from enemy threats, needed a base first.

When the Alaska appropriation finally passed a year later, concern for the security of Alaskans was not what moved the bill. The compelling reason was the fear that Japan would attack Alaska, establish air bases there, and thus bring mainland industrial cities within range of enemy bombers.

In June 1940, the first new Army contingent arrived. The troops started clearing land for an air base on old homestead properties just outside of Anchorage. Again a tent city went shooting up,

✧

Military planes were active in Anchorage prior to and during WWII.

COURTESY OF THE ANCHORAGE MUSEUM OF HISTORY AND ART (B84.51.24).

and, by the end of the month, the first of the fighting troops arrived. Four hundred men and 16 officers got off the train from Seward and marched to their tent encampment, which today is Elmendorf Air Force Base.

One month later, General Simon Bolivar Buckner, Jr., arrived in Anchorage to take command of the Alaska army. Buckner, a former commanding officer at West Point, struck many as belligerent and possibly a braggart. But as the town got to know him, they detected he had a genuine affection for Alaska. He became an expert in training the army to operate in hostile weather and terrain. He built a system of roads that helped connect Anchorage to the 1,630-mile Alaska Highway, which the army finished in 1942, finally ending the territory's isolation from the outside world.

Friends say Buckner confided that he wanted to make Anchorage his home after the war. In speeches to civic clubs, he tried to impress the need for planned development and zoning in Anchorage, which he said, had the potential to become one of the nation's most beautiful cities. He also talked of making a try at running for governor. But an enemy shell ended those dreams. General Buckner was killed in action at the invasion of Okinawa as World War II was winding down.

Today, the Buckner Physical Center, a huge indoor sports arena at Fort Richardson memorializes his name. The airfield itself was named after Captain Hugh M. Elmendorf, who was killed testing new aircraft for the army air corps. It is part of Fort Richardson, the massive army base built virtually next door on the withdrawn wilderness land after the air strip was laid. That facility honors General Wilds P. Richardson, chairman of the Alaska Road Commission, which built the Richardson Highway connecting Fairbanks to Valdez.

The arrival of troops in Anchorage was followed by trainloads of carpenters, plumbers and other skilled craftsmen, plus trainloads of lumber and cement. They mounted a crash program to build the hangars and service buildings at Elmendorf. At the height of construction in the summer of 1941, the government employed 3,415 civilians to work on military construction and at wages averaging about ninety cents an hour, about fifty percent more than the railroad had been paying.

With the defense imperative, Anchorage became Alaska's newest and biggest boom town. Within two years population nearly quadrupled, from 4,000 in 1940 to 15,000 in 1942. The federal government had chosen Anchorage as the military center of Alaska and that established the city as the political and economic center as well.

But boom times again brought familiar problems. Real estate prices skyrocketed. Rent gouging occurred everywhere as contractors and military families tried to grab every empty space. Even garages and sheds were converted into living spaces, often at outrageous rents. Schools were overcrowded, consumers had to scramble—and in some cases mothers had to beg for milk—while store shelves were stripped of goods almost as soon as a new trainload arrived.

Police could not keep up with mounting crime. Big time gamblers moved in, a red light district popped up next to the base in Mountain View, and Anchorage residents reluctantly began locking their doors at night. Some families arranged to send children to schools out-of-state. A good many older residents simply packed their belongings and left.

However, the worst was yet to come.

Chapter VI

On December 7, 1941, as soon as the news spread that the Japanese were bombing Pearl Harbor, Anchorage became a war zone. Sirens screamed and booming cannons signaled all military personnel to return to base. Soldiers and civilian air raid wardens rushed to their posts. Meanwhile, rumors spread that a Japanese air carrier had moved up to the coast of Alaska and that its planes would bomb Anchorage as soon as the weather cleared.

There were few heroes in this moment of panic. Augie Hiebert, a young radio operator in Fairbanks, was certainly one. His actions placed Anchorage on alert well before the military here knew what was happening. Augie wasn't even supposed to be on duty when he heard an announcer break into a scheduled program with a news flash: "Japanese planes are bombing Pearl Harbor." Augie called Colonel Dale Gaffney, commander of Ladd Air Force Base outside Fairbanks. Gaffney then called General Buckner at Fort Richardson in Anchorage. That gave both posts a head start to mobilize, because neither was officially notified of the attack until two hours later.

Some months would pass before the Japanese did attack Alaskan soil. However, for all purposes, Anchorage residents were immediately restricted as though they were in an active war front. Travel in or out of Alaska was promptly sealed off. Steamships were ordered into the nearest ports and airplane pilots had to undergo screening before they could fly.

Life in Anchorage was constantly disrupted by air raid alerts, blackouts, and power shortages. Even after travel barriers were lifted, restrictions harsher than any imposed on the lower forty-eight

✧

Troops land on Attu in the campaign to shove the Japanese from American soil.
COURTESY OF THE ANCHORAGE MUSEUM OF HISTORY AND ART (B50.75.27).

were put into effect. Censors read outgoing and incoming mail. Some newspapers and magazines arrived with holes cut into them, indicating that censors thought certain articles and pictures were subversive, even though they passed muster in the states.

Anchorage residents did have the most to fear. The government had made it the military center of the territory and it had no roads that led anywhere, much less evacuation routes. At the time of Pearl Harbor, the military base had only a few obsolete bombers and a dozen pursuit planes to protect it. Territorial Governor Ernest Gruening publicly tried to prevent panic but inwardly, as he later wrote, he knew the army in Anchorage and elsewhere was totally confused, "running about like chickens with their heads cut off."

It was not until June 3, 1942, about six months after Pearl Harbor, that the Japanese did attack Alaska, but they targeted the distant Aleutian chain, not Anchorage, as had been expected. They took possession of Attu Island and landed troops on Kiska, the first time in 129 years that an enemy had occupied American soil. While the entire American nation seemed shocked, many in Anchorage seemed relieved. The invaders were on a god-forsaken island without an airstrip fifteen hundred miles away, too far to do much harm to Anchorage.

However, Alaska was now an actual war

zone and many more Anchorage families headed for steamship ticket offices. With more than two dozen Japanese submarines reportedly prowling the North Pacific, the evacuating masses actually risked greater danger than those who stayed behind. Fortunately, the Japanese did not attack the passenger ships. The war in Alaska was contained in the far-off Aleutians.

How the United States finally recaptured the Aleutians in the summer of 1943, about a year after the invasion, remains a case study of military miscalculation and fumbling. The people of Anchorage were misled more than others before this debacle ran its course. News blackouts kept them from knowing what was happening in the Aleutians. When the retaking of Kiska was finally disclosed a week after it happened, the military then used the press to try to cover up the blunders. An estimated eighty-five hundred Japanese soldiers were killed, the press release stated, when, in fact, the Japanese had already evacuated the island without the military knowing it. Some 313 American soldiers died, mainly because they were shooting at one another in the fog.

The war was particularly hard on many Alaska residents in other ways. In Anchorage, the populace was particularly incensed by the hysteria to remove Japanese aliens and citizens from the West Coast. Harry Kimura,

an Anchorage pioneer and his talented, much-admired family, were routed out of bed at night and shipped off to detainment camps. Harry, who came to Anchorage in 1916, ran a laundry that washed clothes for the military, and the family operated a popular restaurant. Compounding the indignity, it mattered not that the Kimuras were patriotic citizens. Their oldest son left his job to join the U.S. Army as soon as war broke out.

Of all of the family adjustments made by the stress of war, one in particular stands out in context of Anchorage history. In 1943, health began to fail Edward Anton Rasmuson, a Sweden-born missionary and self-educated attorney, who had controlled the Bank of Alaska for the past twenty-five years. He had developed the bank from a tiny, corrugated iron shack in Skagway in 1918 into a formidable financial empire with branches spreading across Alaska.

Rasmuson had weathered the heavy losses of the Depression and the long hours of those short-handed months when World War II deprived him of stable personnel. But by 1943, his energy was sapped and his health dangerously impaired. He wired his son, Elmer, then on the East Coast, to return to Alaska and relieve him.

Harvard-educated Elmer, then thirty-four, had a promising career as a tax accountant with a prestigious New York firm. He enjoyed his work and the regular weekends of sailing on Long Island Sound. However, he sensed the desperation of his father's call and returned to Alaska.

When Elmer succeeded his father as president of the Bank of Alaska in 1943, one of his first decisions was to move headquarters of the bank from Skagway to Anchorage. It was obvious, as he put it, that "the financial tail was wagging the dog."

His second important decision was to make his bank a member of the Federal Deposit Insurance Corporation, thus removing the competitive advantage of Warren Cuddy's First National Bank. First National's early FDIC accreditation enabled it to grow much faster during the war boom, because the military and the railroad did business only with government-insured banks. Rasmuson's moves

accelerated Anchorage's rise toward becoming the financial center of Alaska

World War II also created a permanent change in the way people in Anchorage traveled. The development of sophisticated aircraft to fight the war led to the development of sophisticated planes for civilian travel. By 1950 the airplane replaced the steamship as the basic means of transporting people and goods.

With the strong editorial and personal support of Bob Atwood at the *Anchorage Times*, Anchorage waged a campaign that won its

✧

Top: Japanese bombs set Dutch Harbor afire June 3-4, 1942.
COURTESY OF THE ANCHORAGE MUSEUM OF HISTORY AND ART (B80.75.13).

Above: Harry Kimura, a revered long-time Alaskan, was subjected to one of the great injustices of World War II.
COURTESY OF THE ANCHORAGE MUSEUM OF HISTORY AND ART (B00.3).

airport the Civil Aeronautics Board's approval to become a port of call on a new North Pacific Route from New York to Chicago to Tokyo, bypassing the traditional stop in Seattle.

The defense department permitted the international flights to use the air force runways at Elmendorf. When that began to create traffic problems with military planes, Atwood and the city's businessmen went into action again. In Washington, they convinced influential military leaders, notably U.S. Air Force Chief of Staff General Carl Spaatz, who used to visit Alaska to hunt, that the government should build an international airport at Anchorage.

Alaska delegate to Congress Bob Bartlett introduced the bill. After the huge facility was built in 1951 at a cost of $12 million, Anchorage proudly laid claim to being the air crossroads of the world. No longer was Anchorage at the mercy of the limited service offered by the unregulated bush pilots. No longer did Anchorage passengers bound for Seattle have to fly to Juneau and try to catch a Pan American plane en route from Fairbanks to Seattle. Now they could board a Northwest plane and fly directly to Seattle or even bypass that city and go on to Chicago or New York.

Anchorage is about equidistant from the bustling manufacturing centers on the East Coast and the major industries in Japan and mainland Asia. At the start of the new century,

the airport was renamed the Ted Stevens Anchorage International Airport in honor of Alaska U.S. Senator Stevens, who, as chairman of the Senate Appropriations Committee, effectively sought federal money to meet the airport's expansion needs.

With landing strips and facilities capable of handling the largest planes, Anchorage became a junction point for international flights directly to the Orient, in effect opening new routes for trade and commerce. In 1999 it served more all-cargo, aircraft-landed weight than any other airport in the nation.

CHAPTER VII

When the war ended, many in Anchorage feared another bust would follow the boom. The government suspended all military construction, putting thousands of well-paid workers out of jobs. About 100,000 of the 150,000 troops brought to Alaska were sent home. As headquarters of the Alaska military command, Anchorage would be hit hardest by the job cuts and troop reductions.

Anchorage did suffer, but not the way most expected. Instead of reeling from the exodus of people, the most pressing problem after the war was how the civilian government of this stressed-out city could sustain an infrastructure for the people who wanted to stay. Many of the military were enchanted by Alaska and opted to retire here or start new careers. The generous homesteading provisions for ex-GIs attracted others. And now that travel barriers were lifted, the city anticipated the waves of tourists blocked so long by the war from hunting, fishing, or just viewing this state's awesome sights.

Of course, a good number of undesirables also chose to stay. Many seamy characters—convicts on the lam, dishonorably discharged soldiers, and even the mentally deranged—moved in during the railroad and wartime booms. Big time racketeers running high stakes games had arrived. So did new batches of prostitutes, violating the tacitly tolerated acceptable number. Token police raids occurred, but it was common knowledge that police from top to bottom were on the take and even fought one another for a share of the graft.

✧

After the war, young families found new homes in Nunaka Valley, where the suburbs of Anchorage expanded.

✧

The damaged but salvaged oil tanker, the
SS Sacketts Harbor, *generated badly*
needed electric power from its berth in the
Port of Anchorage.
COURTESY OF THE ANCHORAGE MUSEUM OF
HISTORY AND ART (MCC-ANCH-DOCKS & HARBORS).

The city jail, with only twenty-nine cells, overflowed after the war. At first, businessmen pooled money so police could send problem criminals on a one-way trip to Seattle. When funds ran out, they tried to deport twenty-three bums with one-way tickets to Seward. However, Seward's mayor got wind of the plan. He met the train, bought them all return tickets, and sent the outcasts back to Anchorage.

Decent housing ranked with crime as major problems, but persistent power shortages were even more critical. The first power station, in Eklutna, had been built to

serve a city of ten thousand. The population was twice that at the end of the war. Outages had become so common that the *Anchorage Times* editorially urged people to turn off needless lights and refrain from opening doors on their ovens to heat their homes.

Here is where Lieutenant Bob Logan, a salvage officer in the navy, deserves a hero's place in Anchorage history. In investigating the wreck of the SS *Sacketts Harbor*, an oil tanker foundering near Adak, he found that the front end had sunk but the stern, containing a virtually undamaged power generating unit, was still afloat. Logan proposed that the stern be salvaged and towed to Anchorage, where the city could plug into its generators.

In October 1946 Logan maneuvered that floating hunk of ship through the turbulent waters of the Shelikof Strait and docked it at low tide in a trench dug in the mudflats off Anchorage harbor. For the next nine years, the vessel generated an average thirty-five hundred KWH daily, meeting the emergency power needs of the city until the Bureau of Reclamation built a huge hydroelectric plant at Eklutna.

The city was not nearly as lucky in solving the housing problem. Almost no houses were built in the years that power was so precarious. This opened the door for an impatient Walter J. Hickel. The son of a Kansas tenant farmer, Hickel, an amateur boxer barely out of high school, sensed at an early age that the farms were blowing away in Kansas and he had to look elsewhere for his future.

In the fall of 1940, at the age of twenty-one, Hickel set off for Alaska, arriving in Anchorage with thirty-seven cents in his pocket. He worked as a dishwasher, as a laborer in the railroad boiler house, and as a bartender. His biggest single payday was a $125 purse he picked up beating a favored boxer in an event tucked between the dogsled races during a Fur Rendezvous, the city's winter carnival.

His life began to stabilize with his marriage to Ermalee Strutz, daughter of a pioneering Alaska family, who was a secretary at Fort Richardson. Between the two, they managed to save enough money to buy a partially built frame house. In finishing it, Hickel learned a lot about carpentry, plumbing, and electrical wiring. He says he felt he had found a vocation.

He sold the house in 1947 and used the money to build three houses to sell at Fireweed and Spenard, just on the outskirts of town. However, the city refused hookups to Anchorage power or water because the buildings were just across the city line. Infuriated, Hickel was forced to build his own generator and water system. He cussed the ineptness of city government and particularly

✦

Nunuka Valley suburbs filled vast acres of open land with new dwellings to accommodate the population influx of the 1950s.

COURTESY OF THE ANCHORAGE MUSEUM OF HISTORY AND ART (WWS-1715-2).

Mayor Z. J. Loussac. That brush with City Hall created another dimension of Walter Hickel. His next battle would not be in the ring, but in the political arena.

With the opening of the Alaska Highway, Hickel was convinced Anchorage badly needed new housing. He went on to form a partnership with a friend, Emil Phiel, a German immigrant, and in two years they built forty-eight rental units. This was the start of the Hickel Construction, which was to have a crucial role in the development of modern Anchorage.

✤

Soggy fairways and all, Anchorage entertained Los Angeles Chamber of Commerce golfers in an early bid for tourism, touting "the most northerly golf course in North America and perhaps in the world."

COURTESY OF THE ANCHORAGE MUSEUM OF HISTORY AND ART (B92.16.1).

The start of Hickel's political career occurred almost by accident. In the fall election of 1950, Loussac ran for the state senate. His opponents heard that Hickel was still burning mad over his treatment at City Hall. They persuaded Hickel to do one radio spot criticizing the mayor.

Hickel accused Loussac of being an absentee mayor, of reneging on election promises by increasing sewer assessments, and of bungling the gravity water system ("we have new pipe but not a drop of water"). Further, he charged Anchorage development was stymied because the city invited needless lawsuits by developers trying to get permits.

No one expected such powerful oratory out of the carpenter. The radio spot was to run only one time, but the delighted sponsors played it eight more times. Loussac lost the election. Hickel and Loussac did some years later patch their differences and become friends. But whether the territory knew it or not, a political star in Alaska was born at that moment in Anchorage.

Hickel joined the Republican Party at a time the state was dominated by Democrats. He would become governor of Alaska twice, and Richard Nixon tapped this self-made, blunt-speaking character to join his cabinet as secretary of interior in 1968. Ironically, Hickel's bluster also proved his undoing in Washington. Nixon fired him two years later after Hickel publicly voiced his opinion that the diviseness over the Vietnam War was tearing the country apart.

However, even during those years of state and federal political success, Hickel never lost touch with Anchorage development. He urged that the city build with vision. "Forget about today. Think about tomorrow," became his byword. As later events showed, he practiced what he preached.

The fortunes of the Hickel Construction Co., among many others, soared with the coming of the Cold War between the United States and Russia. The government again placed Alaska on the front line of American defense, and once more the many millions poured into the state caused Anchorage's economy to explode. Besides expanding Fort Richardson and the Elmendorf Air Force Base, the government also built the DEW line and White Alice communication system across the north to detect approaching Soviet bombers. As the rail and air transportation center of the territory, Anchorage was a second home to thousands traveling to and from their jobs.

In the five years leading up to 1954, military and civilian construction in Anchorage totaled about $375 million, about eighty-five percent of which was publicly funded. This economic burst tripled both the population and the assessed value of property in Anchorage. Already the state's military and economic center, Anchorage now replaced Juneau as the territory's banking center. By 1951, about half of all bank deposits in Alaska were held in Anchorage.

HISTORIC ANCHORAGE

36

CHAPTER VIII

Up to the mid-1950s, the development of Anchorage still pretty much followed the course of the West. Its economy took off every time a huge amount of federal money showed up. However, a new resource discovery in 1957 induced private investors to set off a flood of new income that would further alter the remaining frontier veneer of Alaska's largest city.

The first Alaska oil well capable of producing oil in commercial quantities occurred because of the faith—or luck, some say—of a small group of Anchorage businessmen. Fourteen men who regularly gathered and gabbed during lunch at the downtown Elks Club decided to put up a modest pool of money to buy oil leases with the hope of attracting a major oil company into the territory. Dubbed the "Spit and Argue Club," reportedly by the Elks bartender, the diverse group included publisher Bob Atwood, his banker brother-in-law Elmer Rasmuson, hotelman Wilbur Wester, and Locke Jacobs, Jr., an Army-Navy store clerk. Jacobs was the mastermind of this strange coalition. He kept a daily record of leases filed at the Bureau of Land Management, enabling him to spot the locations where big oil companies were looking.

By mid-April 1955 the group had so many leases that it was approaching its legal limit on acreage. It had barely enough left when it leased one last site—the land around the Swanson River, about thirty-five miles southwest of Anchorage. After waiting futilely for a major oil company to

✧

Capping a long struggle, the Alaska Statehood Committee pauses for a photograph in 1959. Chairman Robert Atwood (background, right) holds the state flag, emphasizing the North Star, which stands for the future of Alaska. E. L. Bartlett, territorial delegate to Congress, holds the left side of the flag. Seated are (from left to right) William Baker, Mildred Hermann, Frank Peratrovich, Percy Ipalook, Warren A. Taylor, Victor Rivers, and Andrew Nerland. Standing next to Atwood is Barrie White, president of Operation Statehood.

COURTESY OF THE ANCHORAGE MUSEUM OF HISTORY AND ART (BL85.63.515).

✧

Above: The first commercially productive oil well in Alaska was discovered at Swanson River in the Kenai Peninsula.
COURTESY OF THE ANCHORAGE MUSEUM OF HISTORY AND ART (MCC 9117).

Below: Governor Ernest Gruening stands in front of the Ship of State plane before leading the statehood lobbying delegation to Washington in 1949.
COURTESY OF THE ANCHORAGE MUSEUM OF HISTORY AND ART (MCC PEOPLE).

knock on their door, the group finally decided to offer their leases free to any company that promised to drill on their site.

Richfield Oil, one of the smallest of the majors, accepted the offer, though insisting as a matter of company policy on providing a five percent override if oil was discovered. Led by geologist drill master William Bishop, Richfield struck a gusher on the Swanson River patch on July 15, 1957. It was a remarkable discovery. In the preceding forty years,

165 consecutive dry holes had been drilled in the search for oil in Alaska.

Together with a three-inch banner headline proclaiming the news, the *Anchorage Times* editorialized: "Hang on, Alaska is going around a sharp curve and is starting down a new road of development such as never has been seen before."

The prediction was correct. The Bureau of Land Management in downtown Anchorage became a madhouse. The news pulled miners from their mines and housewives from their kitchens. Filings for oil leases poured in so fast that Virgil Seiser, the embattled land office manager in Anchorage, was castigated by impatient throngs because his office staff could not keep up with the paperwork The backlog of unrecorded leases even prompted some to call for a congressional investigation.

Meanwhile, just about every major oil company rushed to Alaska looking for oil. More than a dozen of them established headquarters in Anchorage. Standard Oil built the first office building rising above the skyline downtown, a six-story structure at Sixth and Cordova Streets. After court challenges and congressional outbursts ran their course, Swanson River oil exploration boomed. By the mid-1960s, multiple wells in the area were producing 28,500 barrels of oil a day. And off-shore drilling and natural gas development was still ahead.

As the headquarters city for the oilmen, Anchorage now added one more distinction. By 1960 it had become the center of Alaska's budding petroleum industry. Meanwhile, oil royalties and lease sales started to make all Alaska rich.

The Swanson discovery assumed even greater significance than adding private enterprise into the growth of Anchorage. It provided a clinching argument that backers of statehood had lacked for so long. It proved that Alaska now had the resources to make it worthy of statehood.

The statehood movement was spearheaded by Anchorage leaders, essentially in the living room meetings at Bob Atwood's house at 534 L Street. Territorial Governor Ernest Gruening, an avid New Deal Democrat appointed by President Franklin Roosevelt, had

change. The older cities—Fairbanks, under the tight control of Lathrop, and Juneau, content with developing as the capital, which was virtually stolen from Sitka—both liked their lucrative status quo.

The *Anchorage Daily Times* was the first in Alaska to campaign for statehood, staking its position back in 1943. With the discovery of oil at Swanson River, it was now possible to mount a serious push on Congress, and the Anchorage pro-statehood group took the cue.

Atwood's newspaper drew national attention to Alaska's grievances—taxation without representation, decimation of salmon stocks by fish traps placed at the mouths of rivers by profit-driven absentee owners, and ruthless exploitation of mining resources by the likes of the Guggenheims. Atwood said his editorials about the wrongs inflicted by outsiders on this territorial colony grew bolder after each meeting with Governor Gruening.

Alaskans first voted for statehood in 1946. As the new economic boost from the Swanson River oil discovery fueled a new statehood offensive, Alaska could also point with pride to the accomplishments of its constitutional convention, which, in the eyes of respected scholars, produced one of the best constitutions

publicly espoused that the United States hold no colonies. He impressed Atwood, an avid Republican, and became the publisher's mentor during the many meetings at Atwood's home.

Anchorage was a logical place for the statehood movement to flourish. The free-wheeling spirit of this young, fast-growing city had no imbedded prejudices against

Above: Boxer, contractor, and "can-do" developer Walter Hickel (right) takes the oath as governor.
COURTESY OF THE ANCHORAGE MUSEUM OF HISTORY AND ART.

Left: Robert Atwood presided over a statehood victory banquet in Anchorage.
COURTESY OF THE ANCHORAGE MUSEUM OF HISTORY AND ART. PHOTO BY STEVE MCCUTCHEON (MCC 9117).

ever written. But backers still had to convince a Congress that had voted down statehood bills in seven previous sessions.

Gruening developed the master plan to approach Congress. He created national pressure by rounding up a list of prominent Americans, as well as major newspapers, to support statehood. He appointed an Alaska Statehood Committee with Atwood as chairman to carry the fight to Congress and even the White House. Those Alaskans knocked on the door of every congressman whose vote was crucial. Of all the stories of that campaign, Atwood's end run to get into the White House and talk statehood with a skeptical President Dwight Eisenhower stands as an epic in Alaska history.

On June 30, 1958, the Senate passed the statehood bill, clearing the final obstacle in Congress. In August, Alaskan voters approved the three stipulations in the Statehood Act. On January 3, 1959, President Eisenhower signed the proclamation formally marking the admission of Alaska to the Union as the forty-ninth state.

The victory led elated Alaskans to predict that great economic expansion was ahead. The businesses and institutions previously reluctant to invest in a territory could now do so directly with state officials instead of pandering to federal bureaucrats. As the economic center of the new state, expectations ran highest in Anchorage. However, no one could foresee the catastrophe just ahead that would smother the euphoria.

CHAPTER IX

The most powerful earthquake ever recorded in North America struck Anchorage about 5:30 p.m. on March 27, 1964, Good Friday. The shock waves lasted about five minutes, but the devastation of those few minutes changed Anchorage forever.

Many communities in south central Alaska were hit hard, but Anchorage suffered more property damage than the rest of the state combined. Major portions of downtown were wrecked. A stretch of fourteen blocks on the north side of Fourth Avenue, the city's main paved commercial artery, had collapsed. The new five-story JCPenney building, a symbol of the emerging new Anchorage, was damaged beyond repair.

Powerful temblors undermined Turnagain Heights-by-the-Sea, site of the city's finest and most expensive new residential development. The modern houses built on the bluff were swallowed into parting earth and became piles of debris sliding toward the sea. Banker Elmer Rasmuson told of going down a thirty-foot hole to knock a window from his fallen house so he could rescue his dog. Bob Atwood wrote of practicing his trumpet and fleeing when he saw walls starting to bend. He watched his house disappear in a guttural rumble but recovered to lead a party of surviving neighbors, eight women and children, out of the jagged crevasse into which their homes had sunk.

✧

A confused dog searches for his home in
earthquake rubble in the Turnagain suburb.
COURTESY OF THE ANCHORAGE MUSEUM OF
HISTORY AND ART. PHOTO BY WARD WELLS (WW4178-1).

In first reports, the quake registered 8.4 on the Richter scale. It was upgraded later to 9.2 and geologists estimated that it released ten million times more energy than the nuclear bomb dropped on Hiroshima. It killed 114 people across Alaska. While only nine died in Anchorage, it left about two thousand people homeless in the city. Damage to Anchorage's total developed worth was calculated at an amazing seventy-five percent.

While power was quickly restored in much of the city, small tremors continued for days after the big jolt. Some self-certified prognosticators added to the anxiety in radio interviews warning that another earthquake of the same intensity could happen at any moment. Many frightened people simply salvaged what they could and moved out.

The federal government acted swiftly to send relief teams to survey the city's needs, but its help at first actually compounded the uncertainty gripping the city. One of their first studies concluded that downtown land had sunk into graben and was permanently unstable. Even respected citizens talked about moving the city elsewhere.

That a modern, even healthier Anchorage rose from the ashes is an urban miracle. Fortunately, in those moments of panicky undercurrents, several strong leaders came forth to save the city. The first of these was Walter J. Hickel, the former Kansas farm boy, who by now had a reputation as a risk-taking developer.

Sixty days after the earthquake, while civic leaders were pondering the gloomy prospect of whether to move the downtown, Hickel announced he was going to build a high rise

Left: Mac's Photo owner Steve McCutcheon said "We will survive" by posting an optimistic sign in the aftermath of the earthquake.
COURTESY OF THE ANCHORAGE MUSEUM OF HISTORY AND ART (MCC16006).

Below: Emergency crews rushed to search for survivors as soon as the rumbling ceased.
COURTESY OF THE ANCHORAGE MUSEUM OF HISTORY AND ART. PHOTO BY WARD WELLS (WWS 4178-26).

CHAPTER IX

43

hotel called the Captain Cook. right on the risky ground. Some thought he was crazy. Few knew that in searching for building sites earlier in his contracting career, Hickel had paid a soil engineer to analyze Anchorage terrain. "I knew we had stable soil downtown," Hickel told friends.

Obviously, no bank in Alaska was inclined to finance a ten-story building on suspect terrain. Even if they had the courage to do so, each had a lending limit of $30,000. But Hickel found a true believer in Warren Cuddy of the First National Bank in Anchorage. Cuddy introduced him to the president of the Seattle First National Bank. The $4-million Captain Cook Hotel was finished nine months later, financed by Seattle First. Some thirteen years later, Hickel built an even taller companion edifice, a seventeen-floor high rise. This $47-million project also was financed by Seattle First.

The twin towers of the Captain Cook Hotel loom on the Anchorage skyline as impressively as the twin towers do in New York's financial district. Further, the hotel is a lasting symbol of one man's courage to prove that a better city can rise even from nature's worst ravages. In those post-earthquake months when many faced the decision to rebuild or pull out, the confidence which Hickel's gamble restored to others is incalculable. More than $25 million in new building permits were issued in the following year alone. And JCPenney also rebuilt downtown.

Ironically, a second figure worthy of hero status in earthquake recovery lived four thousand miles away. He was President Lyndon Johnson. Reacting to U.S. Air Force photos of the damage, Johnson quickly sent Senator Clinton Anderson of New Mexico, a friend of Alaska in the statehood showdown,

to rush relief efforts. It seemed Johnson instructed Hickel and his commission to act quickly and damn the expense. The federal infusion for recovery was estimated at between $300 million and $400 million, uncommonly generous some say.

Much of the federal outlay had to go to moving the Valdez Port and Business Center to a safer location. The savage tsunami after the quake hit Valdez the worst, washing out the entire commercial center. But government generosity also took good care of crippled Anchorage. The Federal Housing Administration excused mortgage debts on damaged homes with the payment of $1,000. To help citizens finance home repairs, the Small Business Administration made thirty-year loans at three percent interest. Meanwhile, uncalculated millions were spent repairing schools, roads, water and sewer system damages.

President Johnson's swift decisions gave Alaskans both the means and the courage to rebuild. In two years the nearly mortally wounded City of Anchorage was transformed into a fresh-looking metropolis, worthy of the All-American City award it won in 1965 for its remarkable recovery.

Elmer Rasmuson, president of the National Bank of Alaska, has won an honored place in Anchorage history for several reasons, but few connect his name with the important groundwork he laid for the future city after the federal relief teams pulled out. Before the earthquake, this East Coast-oriented son of Alaska served inconspicuously as the first chairman of the Anchorage Planning Commission, a toothless agency, since zoning enforcement was nil.

After seeing his city in disarray, Rasmuson sensed an opportunity for Anchorage to shed its frontier mentality. Since his arrival in 1943, he had watched the city grow haphazardly without a real plan. The people choosing to build in the outskirts to escape city taxes and regulations had organized into a borough and also sprawled in their own haphazard way. Each had its own fire department, and other services were duplicated. The constant tug of war over which entity paid for what scared off developers.

Rasmuson saw a chance to tie in reconstruction with a long range plan for a modern Anchorage, and he decided to run for mayor in 1964 to pursue his mission. Once elected, despite a pitiful mayor's salary of $200 a month, Rasmuson cut back his bank duties and worked full time directing the emergence of a new city. Then he lent his name and his energy in the subsequent campaign to merge the city and borough into a single municipality.

The first two elections to unify lost, largely because the swelling population of voters on the outskirts opposed the merger. Some voted

✧

The Captain Cook Hotel nearing completion on a downtown site that many feared was unsafe.

COURTESY OF THE ANCHORAGE MUSEUM OF HISTORY AND ART. PHOTO BY WARD WELLS (WWS4269).

it down because of fear of higher taxes while others felt a strong loyalty to borough chairman John Asplund, who headed the Spenard Public Utility District and built sewers where the city would not. Finally, in 1972, a unification supporter, John R.Roderick, a Yale graduate, was elected as borough mayor, replacing Asplund as the chief borough officer.

With Roderick's support, the unification charter was approved by about seventy percent of the voters on September 11, 1976. In the election for the first mayor of the Municipality of Anchorage, two respected unification backers faced off. City Mayor George Sullivan, a trucking company operator, defeated Borough Mayor Roderick, a lawyer.

In creating the Municipality of Anchorage, several outlying communities swelling from the influx of workers attracted by the Prudhoe Bay oil discovery and pipeline construction

also became part of Anchorage. With the addition of Eagle River, Chugiak, and Girdwood, Anchorage covered 1,958 square miles, "one of the largest U.S. cities in area," as the *World Book Encyclopedia* describes it.

Considering the competing services and rival labor unions, unifying into a municipality created many administrative problems. However, Anchorage finally had the structure to grow under the long range plan which Rasmuson had envisioned, and Mayor Sullivan seemed to be the right person to enforce that precept.

The municipality dropped the city manager form of government, making Sullivan the first strong mayor. Even in the view of such early critics as publisher Robert Atwood, Sullivan served with distinction for the fourteen years he held office. However, he did have considerable help from the dramatic discovery of undreamed wealth about to flow from the North Slope.

The rebuilt and rejuvenated Anchorage won its second All-American City honors in 1965. It first won the honors in 1956.

COURTESY OF THE ANCHORAGE MUSEUM OF HISTORY AND ART. PHOTO BY WARD WELLS (WWS1848-1).

CHAPTER X

The largest oil field discovery in North America occurred on the remote arctic North Slope in December 1967. Like the earthquake that hit Anchorage three years earlier, its impact also changed the city. It pushed Anchorage into the twentieth century.

Estimates were that the Prudhoe reservoir on the slope contained 5 to 10 million barrels of oil, all on state land. Surely, this would make Alaska fiscally self-sufficient and end the dependence on federal handouts. However, no oil flowed until ten years later. While far away from the oil fields, Anchorage experienced the triumphs and the agonies as Alaska groped and stumbled its way into the oil age.

The most dramatic moment in the jubilant stage occurred in Anchorage on September 10, 1969. The state chose the city for a mammoth sale of North Slope oil leases. Some of the nation's best known journalists—David Brinkley of NBC, Bill Cook of *Newsweek*, and Daryl Lemblo of the *Los Angeles Times*—were among the media seen mingling with the rich and powerful carrying sealed bids for that big day.

✧

The laying of the eight-hundred-mile oil pipeline from Prudhoe Bay to Valdez was one of the greatest engineering feats of the twentieth century.

COURTESY OF THE ANCHORAGE MUSEUM OF HISTORY AND ART. PHOTO BY STEVE MCCUTCHEON.

An overflow audience packed the Sydney Laurence Auditorium and sang the Alaska song while Tom Kelly, commissioner of natural resources, stood by a box guarded by state troopers. As the last notes faded, Kelly reached in and started reading the bids over a loudspeaker. The packed house rocked every time one bid topped another. At the end, the sale yielded $900,220,590, the highest ever realized in any United States oil lease sale.

While the winning oil companies and their contractors rushed machinery and supplies to Fairbanks warehouses, not a shovelful of dirt for the pipeline flew until two time-consuming, major roadblocks were removed. Aboriginal land claims were finally settled with congressional passage of the Alaska Native Claims Settlement Act. Then it took another act of congress to halt the lawsuits by environmental groups alleging that the pipeline project violated provisions of the National Environmental Protection Act.

In 1973, six years after the discovery at Prudhoe, the oil companies were finally cleared to start building the eight-hundred-mile pipeline from the Prudhoe to Valdez. Though still far removed from the pipeline action, Anchorage nevertheless experienced a good share of the agonies of the biggest and wildest boom ever to hit Alaska.

The next three years in Anchorage were as frenzied and uncomfortable as being on another war front. The twenty-five thousand workers building the pipeline picked up big paychecks, most of them making $1,000 a week and some drawing as much as $4,000 weekly. Since only union workers were hired, pipeline job seekers flooded the hiring halls of the Anchorage Teamsters Union, swelling its membership from 9,000 to 23,000 and making Teamster boss Jesse Carr one of the most powerful figures in Alaska.

While workers lived in construction camps on the job, about fifteen thousand of them landed in Anchorage with their hefty paychecks during the three-year construction period. Many sought homes in Anchorage for their families. And those who didn't simply poured into the city for recreation, which included getting drunk,

raising hell, visiting the waiting ladies at Spenard, or all of the aforementioned. Prices for homes tripled. Finding an apartment or house to rent became next to impossible. High stakes gambling and its attendant crime flourished.

Oil finally began to flow in 1977. Now rewards overshadowed the agonies. Through hard campaigning by city fathers, supported by Atwood's editorials, the largest companies pumping oil out of the North Slope chose to locate their headquarters in Anchorage, beating out Fairbanks. Atlantic Richfield (ARCO) built a twenty-one-story office tower of glass and steel downtown at a cost of $65 million. Sohio, British Petroleum's domestic subsidiary, erected a handsomely landscaped fifteen-story midtown tower at a cost of $75 million.

Other players in the oil hunt eagerly joined in removing vestiges of the frontier. Nelson Bunker Hunt built a twenty-story high-rise, at a cost of $45 million, a few downtown blocks away from ARCO. (When Hunt's fortunes fell on hard times in the 1990s, the building was purchased by the State of Alaska.) Lesser high-rises built by oil-related firms sprouted all over the city. Acres

of tiny cottages downtown were bulldozed to make way for a forest of gleaming office buildings, a tragedy in the minds of those who worried about preserving some of the frontier heritage.

Even bigger imprints by the oil boom were still ahead for Anchorage. The torrents of oil flowing down the pipeline provided torrents of cash, an arsenal of money the city never dreamed of having. By 1982, the royalties, severance payments, and corporate taxes from oil pushed state revenues to $4.5 billion a year. Alaska needed only $1 billion to balance the budget. The state spread the excess around lavishly, much of it as direct payments to municipalities.

With nearly half of the state's population living in Anchorage, the city awaited a bonanza of money. The administration of Mayor Sullivan in his final term was the first beneficiary of this oil age gusher. Sullivan pledged to use it to improve the quality of life of the city.

Above: ARCO planted its headquarters in downtown by building a twenty-one story office tower of glass and steel. Since selling its Alaska assets was an anti-trust stipulation of ARCO's merger with British Petroleum, the building now flies the flag of Phillips Alaska, its current owner.

PHOTO BY HAL GAGE © 2001.

Right: The twenty-story Hunt Building, now the Atwood Building, is one of the high-rises built by oil-related businesses after the major producers committed their headquarters to Anchorage.

PHOTO BY HAL GAGE © 2001.

CHAPTER XI

In 1950, Victor Fischer, a recent MIT graduate, arrived in Anchorage to become the city's first planning director. He was hired at the behest of Elmer Rasmuson, who chaired the planning commission. Fischer had no staff but was thrilled by what he saw. While house-hunting, he drove down a little dirt road that led through the spruce and cottonwoods growing just east of Anchorage. He arrived at a knoll and stopped. He looked in awe at the vast acreage of forest, meadow and pools of water below. All untouched by man.

Fischer's first thought was, "This is where I want to build my house." However, the land was government property, off limits to the public. And so it remained, still undisturbed by man, during the four years Fischer served. Anchorage grew at a phenomenal pace during that period—the White Alice and Cold War defense buildup of the 1970s. As the lone paid planner, Fischer had more than he could handle in helping the administration resolve daily zoning disputes and facilitating subdivisions. He could only dream of how that majestic land could fit into the city's future.

The acreage had been acquired by the army but never used for anything during World War II. When the war ended, the military turned over the entire tract of more than 1,000 acres to the War Assets Administration, which declared it surplus. It, in turn, transferred the property to the Bureau of Land Management for use as an "institutional reserve." That now gave non-profit users an opportunity to obtain the land at nominal cost.

The City of Anchorage quickly claimed the Goose Lake park section, where swimmers and nature lovers now share the lake and its wooded surroundings with a thriving moose population. Before leaving in 1955, Fischer worked with a committee of Chamber of Commerce and city

✧

Anchorage's first planning director, Victor Fischer, recalled being awed by the "majestic" surplus of open land available for an Anchorage university/health center complex. This 1953 picture shows Fischer examining the first aerial topographical survey taken of the area.

COURTESY OF THE *ANCHORAGE DAILY NEWS*, *ANCHORAGE TIMES* ARCHIVES.

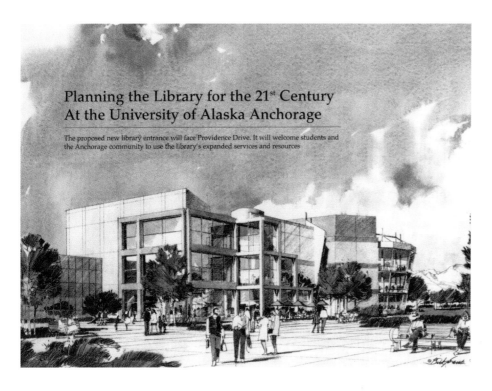

Planning the Library for the 21st Century
At the University of Alaska Anchorage

The proposed new library entrance will face Providence Drive. It will welcome students and the Anchorage community to use the library's expanded services and resources

✧

Above: An artist's rendering of the expanded consortium library serving the University of Alaska and Alaska Pacific University. The library was under construction in 2001.

PHOTO BY HAL GAGE © 2001.

Below: Providence Alaska Medical Center, a $600-million, 322-bed facility, sits in a park-like complex with a religious statue at its entrance.

PHOTO BY HAL GAGE © 2001.

leaders to contact mission-minded religious leaders and try to persuade them to start a college campus on the unclaimed land. As the largest and fastest growing city in Alaska, Anchorage still had no college, but it had all the demographics to support one.

The Methodists were the first, and the only ones, to show an interest. It is widely believed that the church officials pursued the invitation to build only after top administrators of the University of Alaska, which is based in Fairbanks, promised that the state university system would not establish a competing branch campus in Anchorage.

In 1957 Alaska Methodist University was chartered and, through a Bureau of Land Management grant, acquired 242.5 acres of the remaining surplus. By 1960 the AMU began offering classes to Anchorage area students. They had the comfort in knowing that in 1953 the state board of regents voted to expand the university system away from Fairbanks, but only in the form of community colleges. The regents decreed that no new structures would be erected, but community colleges classes would be held in high school classrooms already available.

However, the pressure on the state to extend the university system into Anchorage grew as it was fast becoming the population center. of Alaska. In 1962, two years after

Alaska Methodist opened, the legislature established the Anchorage Regional Center, which began offering four-year college courses. By 1968 the agitation for an Anchorage-based four-year university brought about the birth of the Anchorage Senior College, which in effect created the first University of Alaska Anchorage.

In 1973 the legislature built a Consortium Library on land donated by Alaska Methodist University in exchange for use of the library. Anchorage Community College, UAA and AMU used the library jointly, but the senior college occupied the second floor and taught upper division and graduate classes at tuition considerably lower than Methodist University. This marked the start of the UAA campus.

Despite attempts to permit students to cross-register classes, Alaska Methodist suffered. An unexpected blow was struck when, in 1976, Dr. John Lindauer was brought in as the first chancellor of the University of Alaska, Anchorage, replacing Dr. Lewis Haines, the provost. With oil money about to flow in great torrents, Lindauer's mission seemed to be to elevate state-supported higher education in Anchorage regardless of the alleged promises.

With Lindauer's arrival, Alaska Methodist University closed its doors. It managed to

ALASKA NATIVE MEDICAL CENTER
4315 DIPLOMACY DRIVE

reorganize in 1978 as Alaska Pacific University and in time found its niche as a respected liberal arts non-denominational institution. It retained privileges of the consortium library and grew into an important alternative to those who prefer a private college to a state-run school.

Meanwhile, the Anchorage Community College grew into the largest single educational unit in the entire University of Alaska system. This further increased demands for a next step upper level institution. In 1986 the board of regents brought in Dr. Donald O'Dowd, a prominent east coast educator, to reorganize the entire university system. He quickly merged UAA and ACC into one institution, the University of Alaska Anchorage.

Above: The Alaska Native Medical Center, a $150-million project with 150 beds, was completed in 1997. The campus includes a park-like setting and University Lake.
PHOTO BY HAL GAGE © 2001.

Below: Built by the teamsters union, Alaska Regional Hospital offers modern medical facilities with 254 beds closer to midtown.
PHOTO BY HAL GAGE © 2001.

By the turn of the century, the newly formed university in Anchorage became the giant of the state's university system. Its 428-acre campus of modern buildings and well-landscaped surroundings is attractive to out-of-staters and Alaskans alike. It attracts fifteen thousand students a year, far more than the parent university at Fairbanks.

The majesty of the surplus acreage also impressed other Alaska visionaries, among them developer Wally Hickel. After the earthquake, he saw a chance to do something about overcrowded medical care. The city's lone medical center, Providence Hospital on L Street in downtown, had survived the 1964 earthquake with minor damage, but the rapid population growth had already stressed its facilities.

In the late 1950s, the Sisters of Providence had the foresight to buy a tract of that surplus land in the Goose Lake area. In 1975 Hickel, now with the added prestige of being a former governor and U.S. secretary of interior, rounded a group of civic leaders and led a successful

$3.5-million fund drive to anchor the Providence Alaska Medical Center in the park-like tract and expand the facilities. Since then, the hospital center has grown into a $600-million, 352-bed complex with helicopter service. On the other end of that once-surplus tract, The Alaska Native Medical Center in 1997 built a $150-million project with 150 beds. Closer to midtown, the Alaska Regional Hospital, built by the teamsters in the pipeline boom, was beset by ownership changes, but by the turn of the century it stabilized into a modern medical facility with 254 beds.

The growth of the education system and the presence of a world-class medical care continue to improve the quality of life in Anchorage. Major improvement of the cultural environment was next to develop. That, too, required vision and commitment. It is a story of how a banker, whose favorite sport was sheep hunting, turned into the foremost patron of the arts in Anchorage and all Alaska. It is a story best told by the person himself in the next chapter.

CHAPTER XII

BY ELMER E. RASMUSON

In 1955 a group of Anchorage citizens incorporated the Cook Inlet Historical Society. Leading spirits in this organization were Evangeline Atwood and Herb Hilscher. Other founding members included Bob and Tilly Reeve, Arthur Eide, and Norma Hoyt. Their limited collection was housed in the old City Hall.

During my tenure as mayor of Anchorage, I felt strongly that our community needed a museum in which we could take pride and which would serve as a cultural inspiration for both residents and visitors. Accordingly, I proposed to the City Council that if they would dedicate an available city block, I would raise the money from private sources to construct the first phase of the museum building. The council agreed and to fulfill the obligation, my wife, Mary Louise, and I hosted a luncheon on June 29, 1966, to which we invited a group of citizens who had shown an interest in this project. In attendance at the luncheon were Evangeline and Bob Atwood, Bob Reeve, Norma Hoyt, Herb Hilscher, Dick

✧

Then-Mayor of Anchorage Elmer Rasmuson broke ground for today's museum building in 1967. Others in the picture include (from left to right) Mary Louise Rasmuson, chairman of the advisory committee; Evangeline Atwood; Bill Creighton, director of parks and recreation; Dick Silberer; Bob Reeves; and Wilda Hudson.

✧

Above: A frieze of concrete panels designed and carved by Alex Duff Combs graces the top of the museum building.

COURTESY OF THE ANCHORAGE MUSEUM OF HISTORY AND ART (B01.2.2).

Below: The stunning entrance to the Anchorage Museum of History and Art, c. 1985.

COURTESY OF THE ANCHORAGE MUSEUM OF HISTORY AND ART. PHOTO BY PAUL WARCHOL.

Silberer (representing Wally and Ermalee Hickel), Mary Louise and myself. We estimated the construction cost of $400,000. There was $131,000 available from the Centennial Commission (federal funds), leaving a balance needed of $269,000. Mary Louise and I offered to pledge one half if the guests would pledge the other half, the pledges to be due over a five-year period.

The guests all rose to the occasion, and nobly so. Bob Reeve commented afterwards that this was the most expensive luncheon he ever attended. The ground-breaking ceremony was held on September 12, 1967. Kenneth Maynard was the architect and the Howard S. Lease Company, the builder. Alex Duff Combs designed and carved a frieze of concrete panels. This frieze was originally installed around the top of the building. When the museum was expanded with funds from the state, the panels were preserved as an interior frieze on the second floor.

Additional funds were needed for some overruns plus exhibit facilities and numerous public spirited individuals stepped forward with the necessary funds. These original contributors are all listed as "founders" in the museum records and on the entrance wall of the present structure.

Because there was considerable dual membership among the founders and the Cook Inlet Historical Society and also to be more inclusive in museum mission and exhibits, it was agreed to join forces with the society and the official name was adapted as the Anchorage Museum of History and Art. [*Author's note: Records show that it was first named the Anchorage Historical and Fine Arts*

Museum, but became the Anchorage Museum of History and Art when it opened its doors in 1968.]

Also taking a page out of the successful strategy of Andrew Carnegie in his library program, the founders turned the museum ownership over to the City of Anchorage. This civic ownership provides support for personnel, security, heat and power, etc. It also gives the citizenry of Anchorage a proprietary interest in the museum and continuing support. I believe that this municipal ownership is one of the key reasons for the success of the museum and have urged that a similar strategy be followed by other libraries and museums throughout the state.

The museum opened its doors on July 18, 1968, with an exhibit of borrowed paintings and a collection of twenty-five hundred items from the Cook Inlet Historical Society. Michael Kennedy was the first director. Since the museum is technically a part of the municipality, traditional procedure dictated that there be an official advisory committee. Thus was created the Historical and Fine Arts Commission to be the official liaison between the museum and the mayor and assembly. I appointed Mary Louise to chair the first advisory committee and Mayor George Sullivan appointed her to be the first chairman of the commission. Mary Louise proved to be an able and energetic chairman, and the mayors continued to reappoint her until she retired from that position.

In the year following the formal opening, an extremely important addition to the museum family was created, e.g. the Anchorage Fine Arts Museum Association (AFAMA). [*Author's note: Today, it goes by the name of the Anchorage Museum Association.*] This is a "friends" group designed to provide private support for the museum. It operates the Museum Shop, which raises significant funds for the museum, particularly for acquisitions and traveling exhibits. It is also the organization which individuals join to help the museum. It is truly a vital organization, accountable to a great extent for the success of the museum. The original chairman of the association was Judge James von der Heydt, Saradell Ard, and Robert Ely were on the first board of directors and have continued to serve the museum in various capacities.

In 1973 the voters approved a $1.2 million bond issue to build an addition to the museum. As I remember, all the other proposed bond issues failed, which showed the overwhelming public support that the museum had generated.

In 1981 Mayor George Sullivan and the Anchorage Assembly included the expansion of the museum in a major public facilities construction program known as Project 80s. In 1982 Mayor Tony Knowles continued the municipality's commitment, and the Anchorage voters approved the expansion project. The state funds allocated to this project

total $22.8 million and provided for ninety-three thousand square feet of museum space. To supplement the public funds, private subscriptions raised another $1.7 million.

In 1989 Mary Louise retired from the Museum Commission. However, it was deemed beneficial by museum supporters that a museum foundation be organized to expand sources of revenue for exhibits, for improvement and, particularly, eventual expansion. Mary Louise was elected in 1989 as chairperson of a Museum Foundation Board. This board is composed of an action-minded group of citizenry and at this writing (mid-1998) presides over a fund of $10 million. Ed Rasmuson is chairman of the investment committee with Gail Sieberts as a diligent treasurer and Gary Dalton as active investment advisor.

December 15, 1993, was an important milestone in the history of the museum. On that date, Mayor Tom Fink signed a five-year agreement with representatives of the National Museum of Natural History, a Smithsonian Institution, to establish an Arctic Studies Center. This was the culmination of many years of work by museum officials to interest the Smithsonian in joint efforts. It was the first time that the Smithsonian had entered into a partnership with a local museum. It has not only proved very successful in Alaska but has served as a model for Smithsonian

✧

Above: Saradell Ard was one of the first board members named to the fine arts museum board designed to provide private support for the museum. She joined Judge James von der Heydt, chair, and Robert Ely.
COURTESY OF THE ANCHORAGE MUSEUM OF HISTORY AND ART (B01.2.1).

Below: The dazzling thirtieth anniversary exhibit in July 1998 is typical of the almost non-stop programs and community events offered at the Anchorage Museum of History and Art.
COURTESY OF THE ANCHORAGE MUSEUM OF HISTORY AND ART. PHOTO BY CHRIS AREND.

stimulating enterprises in which we have been privileged to participate. It will continue to be so. In turn we have been very honored. The atrium is named for Mary Louise and in a public ceremony in 1996, led by Mayor Mystrom, the entire block was designated as the Rasmuson Center.

[*Author's note: While this is the end of Elmer Rasmuson's account of the history of the museum, it is far from the end of this success story. On February 15, 1999, at the occasion of his ninetieth birthday, Elmer announced that he was arranging for the transfer of $50 million in stock to the Anchorage Museum Foundation "for purposes of expansion of this museum." Further, he said he also planned a similar transfer of $40 million in stock to the Rasmuson Foundation, which makes support grants to public service organizations on a statewide basis.*

Unfortunately, Elmer did not live to see the expansion. He died December 1, 2000, at the age of ninety-one, soon after he finalized the sale of the National Bank of Alaska, the state's biggest, to San Francisco-based Wells Fargo for $1 billion. He also had assured the orderly transition of administration of the bank. Elmer's son, Edward Rasmuson, well-tutored by his father, was installed as chairman and chief executive officer, the third generation of his family to run the bank.]

✧

Above: Mary Louise Rasmuson and Anchorage Mayor Tony Knowles formally open the atrium at the Anchorage Museum of History and Art in 1996.

COURTESY OF THE ANCHORAGE MUSEUM OF HISTORY AND ART (B99.1.1).

Below: A crowd in 1996 participates in a celebration naming the museum atrium for Mary Louise Rasmuson and designating the entire museum block as the Rasmuson Center.

COURTESY OF THE ANCHORAGE MUSEUM OF HISTORY AND ART. PHOTO BY CHRIS AREND.

participation elsewhere. In July 1998, Robert Fri, director of the NMNH, and Mayor Rick Mystrom signed a twenty-year extension of our partnership agreement. I have high hopes that in the future the Smithsonian will be a close partner and supporter of Alaska museum efforts in both programs and exhibits.

Currently, the four support groups of the museum are working on a program for expansion...Mary Louise and my involvement in the museum has been one of the most

Chapter XIII

The Anchorage Museum of History and Art, now renowned the world over, is a testament to the cultural conscience of those who made their fortunes in Alaska. As streams of oil money began to flow in at the end of the 1970s, that conscientiousness became catching. State and municipal governments were inspired to invest their own riches in arts and recreation, creating a cultural renaissance in Anchorage during the 1980s.

By the start of that decade, oil royalties and commissions from Prudhoe Bay pushed state revenues to $5 billion a year, far more than needed to balance the budget. While the governor and legislature spread the surplus money around lavishly on several outrageous boondoggles in pursuit of the elusive goal to make Alaska economically self-sufficient, they also had the good sense to make direct cash payments to municipalities. The distributions were based on a formula of $1,000 per resident, to be used any way the towns saw fit.

Since about half of the state's 500,000 people lived in Anchorage, the municipality found itself awash in money. True to its promise made to oil companies in persuading them to locate their headquarters there, Anchorage earmarked more than $250 million to cultural amenities toward its goal of becoming a world class city.

The centerpiece of this undertaking, called "Project 80s" was the $75-million Alaska Center for the Performing Arts, which houses three state-of-the art theaters. The largest is the twenty-one-hundred-seat Evangeline Atwood Theater. It is the base for the Anchorage Symphony and accommodates the largest of national attractions. Many star performers, ranging from comics of Jay

✧

The George M. Sullivan Arena is home to ice hockey teams, touring musical shows, trade exhibitions, and the Great Alaska Shootout. It seats eight thousand people.
PHOTO BY HAL GAGE © 2001.

Leno's stature to nationally acclaimed musical organizations such as the San Francisco Opera, regularly appear on its stages, often with high praise for the facility.

The George M. Sullivan Arena, built for $34.5 million, seats eight thousand. Besides accommodating professional and collegiate hockey teams, sportsmen's shows, and various trade exhibitions, it is home each year to the Great Alaska Shootout. Some of the nation's best basketball teams compete in the November tournament, which is nationally televised.

The Egan Civic and Convention Center ($26.8 million) is across the street from the performing arts center and within walking distance of the expanding complex of first-class hotels in downtown. It is the central annual meeting place for the Alaska Federation of Natives convention, and a recently-built skywalk linking it to the arts center makes it a selling point for conventions. Delegates can meet comfortably even in the severest of winters.

The arts have always been lively in Alaska, although much of the fare was homespun, ranging from Native dancing to thespian recitals of *The Shooting of Dan McGrew* at the Malamute Saloon. One of the true cultural pioneers was Lorene Harrison, the first music teacher in Anchorage public schools. She not only directed amateur shows and church choirs, but also instilled a desire for a higher level of performing arts. She was the guiding spirit behind the first Anchorage Concert Association and the Anchorage Community Chorus, the first of the city's many musical associations, which included a symphony orchestra, an opera company, and a civic ballet.

The cultural vigor of Anchorage ascended to new heights with the influx of the people transferred here by the oil companies. The arrival of so many families from Dallas and other sophisticated oil-rich cities from the lower forty-eight provided not only well-heeled patrons of the arts, but many who became dedicated citizens willing to work to improve their new hometown. They even started the Alaska Repertory Theater, acclaimed by national critics as "truly outstanding." Some of the lasting beneficiaries are the half dozen or so theatrical groups that perform at the University of Alaska Anchorage, Alaska Pacific University, and Cyranos. The arts became adventurous, polished, and exceptionally well funded.

Christine D'Arcy, head of the Alaska State Council on the Arts, an allocating agency, described the impact: "The biggest legacy of the oil money was the development of cultural facilities throughout the state. But what also happened was that the arts organizations were able to undertake sustained creative development and hire staffs to promote fund-

✧

Lorene Harrison, the first music teacher in Anchorage, became a pioneer cultural leader, encouraging amateur shows while instilling a desire for a higher level of performing arts.

COURTESY OF LORENE HARRISON.

raising. As a result, today we have a $23-million arts industry that provides income to four thousand people throughout the state."

Many of the transferees were induced to come by substantial financial bonuses from their oil companies. Their investments also became a factor in the changing demographics of Anchorage. The wealthiest built million dollar homes on the mountainsides with spectacular vistas of the Cook Inlet and the Alaska Range. The moderately affluent moved into the blocks of elegant homes and condos, some hastily erected alongside the weather-beaten shacks and trailer courts that housed the earlier generations of Alaskans.

Trendy restaurants, boutiques, and interior decorating shops mushroomed where scrubby brush had stood. The building pace became so frantic that in 1983 alone permits were issued for a billion dollars' worth of construction, exceeding the combined building permits issued in that year to the also thriving cities of Seattle, Portland, and Honolulu. Moneylenders from inside the state and out stormed in, particularly to take advantage of state-guaranteed housing loans.

The swelling population also caught the attention of the wealthy McClatchy newspaper chain based in Sacramento. In 1980, it became a big player in the boom by acquiring the ailing *Anchorage Daily News*, a morning paper which Kay Fanning tried to keep alive after the death of her husband. Pouring millions into a new publishing plant and many millions more into staff, advertising incentives, and circulation promotion, McClatchy set out to overtake Robert Atwood's *Anchorage Times*, long the dominant paper in Alaska.

Atwood capitulated to McClatchy's spending blitz in 1990, selling the *Times* to Bill Allen, whose Veco company had been enriched by winning Exxon's oil spill cleanup contract in Prince William Sound. Allen

invested a small fortune of his own in a newspaper war with McClatchy, but he, too, could not compete against the national newspaper chain. He sold the *Anchorage Times* to McClatchy on June 2, 1992, and McClatchy shut down the venerable *Times* the next day.

Anchorage will not soon forget the impact of another big player in the boom of the 1980s. Peter Zamarello, born to poor Italian parents on the Greek Island of Cephalonia, made his way to Anchorage a step ahead of immigration authorities in the 1960s. He came as a carpenter but quickly learned how

to take advantage of the banks pouring in lending money for building projects. Nearly anybody could get a loan in the sizzling Anchorage real estate market. So Zamarello set aside his hammer and became a builder.

By borrowing, building, and borrowing some more, Zamarello saturated the city with strip malls. Most of his malls and plazas are undistinguished rows of humdrum storefronts strung together under elongated blue roofs. He kept building even when a steep drop in oil prices—from $27 a barrel to less than $10—in 1986 caused other developers to retrench and impelled banks to resort to sterner credit checks because the city was overbuilding. By the end of the year, the Zamarello empire collapsed into a bankrupt mess. Nine of Alaska's fifteen banks went broke or were forced into mergers soon after, most of them overleveraged in real estate and many of them carrying uncollectible loans made to Zamarello.

The business failures in the late 1980s had little lasting impact on Anchorage. The Federal Deposit Insurance Corporation (FDIC) absorbed the biggest hit. The federal government took over $1.5 billion in bad loans and then sold defaulted property at firesale prices. This brought down inflated real estate prices and rentals in what some economists viewed as an overdue correction.

CHAPTER XIV

Life in Anchorage stabilized and steadily improved in the 1990s. The city matured. Gone were the delusions that its frantic rate of expansion would go on forever. Gone was the mind set that the city's destiny rested on the massive subsidies passed on by the price of oil. For this, Anchorage can thank the succession of enlightened leaders that guided the municipality after the shocks of the 1980s.

Tony Knowles, a native Oklahoman with a economics degree from Yale, ascended the political ladder from municipal assembly member to mayor in 1981. While he served during the speculative building boom and its free fall, he managed to see the fragility of the boom and recognize that the city's future lay in improving the quality of life for its residents and visitors.

Aside from channeling money into the big arts and recreation projects of the renaissance years, he created the Anchorage Development Corporation. Also emerging from mayoral-inspired brainstorming was the plan to build trails and bike paths that would reveal the beauty of the hidden vistas of the city. The fourteen-mile Tony Knowles Coastal Trail, much of it overlooking the Cook Inlet, is probably unmatched in any city. Walkers, cyclists, and skiers can enjoy uninterrupted solace from downtown to Kincaid Park, where a cross-country ski trail system and and an indoor sports facility also serve the recreation-minded.

Golfers, horseback riders, skaters, bird watchers, and even trout fishermen benefit from separate park and water recreation areas developed in Anchorage. It was a mark of his compassion, perhaps,

✧

Sled dog races are a major attraction at the winter Fur Rendezvous. In this photo, former Anchorage Mayor George Sullivan is among the participants lining up his dog team for the celebrity race.

Mayor Tony Knowles, an avid jogger,
founded the fourteen-mile park trail that
bears his name.

COURTESY OF TONY KNOWLES.

that Knowles, who was elected governor after two terms as mayor, also initiated programs to help the forgotten people. His support was important in developing the Brother Francis Shelter for the homeless and Bean's Cafe, which provides meals for the dispossessed.

Mayor Rick Mystrom, who ended two terms in 2000, added his own unique ideas in improving the quality of life. He set out to make Anchorage a handsome city. As a public relations expert, Mystrom raised more than $1.5 million in private dollars to build an image of Anchorage as a city of lights and flowers.

The long daylight hours and steady moisture in the summers are ideal for annual planting. Municipal gardeners make Anchorage intersections and planting beds along public buildings a blooming spectacle that awes residents and tourists alike. Many private homeowners pick up the cue and decorate their properties with the begonias, marigolds, and geraniums that thrive here in the summer. The University of Alaska Anchorage gardeners plant as many as fourteen thousand flowering annuals each summer in keeping with the plan.

Winters are long in Alaska, and, in the gloomiest months, daylight comes in mid-morning and lasts only until mid-afternoon. To brighten the long nights, Mystrom next endeavored to make Anchorage the "City of Lights." Residents were urged to keep outdoor lights on all night during the winter. Some responded by leaving their Christmas lights burning until the days grow longer in the spring.

Anchorage long ago established customs designed to break up winters. In 1936 it began a winter festival today known as "Fur Rendezvous." The original purpose was to bring trappers and buyers into town under friendly auspices. They would cut out the middleman as they socialized and bargained over fox, wolf, and beaver pelts. Sixty-five years later that modest winter social has grown into one of the largest winter festivals in North America.

The ten-day celebration of Fur Rondy occurs each February. While a few fur-selling trappers still show up, the festival features 120 fun events, ranging from outhouse racing to championship sled dog races during the day to melodramas by the Anchorage Sourdough Chorus and dancing at the Miners and Trappers Ball at night.

Almost as soon as the festival revelry dies out, Anchorage embraces another big winter event—the Iditarod. The world's top sled racing dog teams line up in the city in early March to begin the 1,049-mile race from Anchorage to Nome. Crowds cheer the dozens of dog teams as they take off to the commands of the musher riding at the rear of the sled.

✧

Moose sightings within the city thrill visitors, but some Anchorage residents complain the animals have become too numerous and residents cannot protect their ornamental shrubs from the animals during the winter.

PHOTO BY JOHN STROHMEYER.

ANCHORAGE
FUR RONDEZVOUS
ESKIMO BLANKET-TOSS

E 55

Only about two-thirds of the teams make it to Nome, but the finishers of "the Last Great Race on Earth" can look to increasing larger rewards. The modest early prizes have grown to a total purse of $550,000 in the year 2001, with $63,000 going to the winner, and the remainder distributed to the other top thirty finishers. The winning racers also collect considerably more from commercial endorsements and appearances.

While some still joke that Anchorage is "only a half hour from Alaska," the fact is that Anchorage maintains many of the ties to nature that make Alaska distinctive. Few cities can offer the prospect of such adventure within the city limits. Moose straying from the parks often stop traffic on city streets. Huge king salmon and acrobatic cohos migrate up Ship Creek so near to downtown that store clerks and proprietors alike walk a few blocks during their lunch hour to cast a line or watch the action. Bears raid garbage bins outside the expensive homes on the hillside.

Further, Anchorage is making a longterm commitment to live with nature. Its comprehensive plan for the year 2020 incorporates "Living with Wildlife," a blueprint prepared by state, federal and city agencies to "conserve, enhance and restore optimal populations of native wildlife and their habitats in the Municipality of Anchorage." In essence, the city seeks to incorporate a plan that includes open spaces where the wilderness is still welcome to call.

While some residents feel the city is already too overrun with nature and take it upon themselves to collect eggs to keep down the Canadian goose population. The concept of preserving open space has support even from people who might appear to have much to gain from more building. The Cuddy family, which controls the First National Bank, a traditional big lender to developers, personally raised $300,000 to save parklike land separating the Loussac Library from encroaching big box retail stores in midtown.

At the turn of this century, many economic changes are affecting Alaskans. Oil production at Prudhoe is declining. Mergers of the largest oil companies are causing trimmed payrolls. Service jobs increase as higher paying ones decline. However, Anchorage has several anchors to the wind. The oil industry is not about to disappear, and its commitment to Anchorage as the headquarters city is firm. The federal government remains a stabilizing employer. The bases alone at Elmendorf and Fort Richardson generate annual payrolls of $250 million for the military and $105 million for the civilian workforce.

Anchorage citizens, like all Alaskans, have the comfort of receiving annual dividend checks, now approaching $2,000 for every man, woman and child, from the Permanent Fund. This is the oil revenue savings account set up to stay out of the reach of the legislature, and at the turn of the century it has grown to $26 billion. However, the greatest comfort may be in watching the phenomenal growth of tourism.

In assessing the future of the city in a piece for the *National Geographic*, Larry King wrote about Anchorage: "It remains one of the earth's few remaining places not tired and used up." Many around the world are willing to travel thousands of miles to feel the charm. In the last annual count, about 1.2 million tourists came to Alaska. Of those, 1.1 million visited Anchorage.

POPULATION

According to U.S. Census figures for the year 2000, the population of Anchorage climbed from 226,338 to 260,283 during the past ten years, a gain of fifteen percent. The number of Alaska Natives living in Anchorage was placed at 18,941, up thirty percent over ten years ago.

All other segments of the city's population also increased in the past decade. Hispanics led the way with a gain of sixty percent, growing from 9,258 to 14,799. Asians and Pacific Islanders grew from 10,910 to 16,856, an increase of fifty-four percent. Caucasians increased by 5,273, or about three percent, to 188,009, and the population of African Americans grew by 655, or five percent, for a total of 15,199.

Overall the population of Alaska stood at 626,932, a gain of 76,899 more people since 1990. It is now only the third smallest state in population, having surpassed Vermont sometime during the 1990s. Wyoming is still the least-populated state.

⟡

By 1940 bustling Fourth Avenue was called "Alaska's Broadway" by some.

SHARING THE HERITAGE

*historic profiles of businesses,
organizations, and families that have
contributed to the development and
economic base of Anchorage*

SPECIAL THANKS TO

AT&T Alascom

ABC Motorhome &
Car Rentals

THE ARC OF ANCHORAGE

The ARC of Anchorage (ARC) is proof positive that caring people can make a difference. A group of a few parents concerned about the education of their children with mental retardation joined together in 1957 and formed the Parents Association for Retarded Children of Anchorage (PARCA). Today, their organization is The ARC of Anchorage—a multi-faceted organization providing fifteen special programs for hundreds of children and adults in Anchorage.

Historically, mentally retarded children and adults were almost always institutionalized at birth. After World War II, a new attitude prevailed, and families began to insist they be allowed to care for their loved ones. The National Association of Retarded Children was formed in 1950 as a way to galvanize the efforts of these parents.

The first goal of the new Alaskan organization was to start education programs for young children. PARCA was able to begin Special Education classes in September 1957, and in January 1958 the Anchorage School District (ASD) provided its first teacher for children with mental retardation.

In 1958 the board of directors of PARCA established goals of acquiring land and constructing a permanent building. These lofty goals could not be realized without enthusiastic fundraising. The making and selling of candles was one of their first projects. "Light a Life" and "Light a Child's Way" were sales themes. The

project quickly spread throughout the community, and soon many were involved. As PARCA grew fundraising efforts grew, too, eventually including bake sales and fashion shows, featuring the individuals in the families of those benefiting from the programs. The first Mayor's Ball in 1969 was started as a fundraiser for the ARC, and in subsequent years has benefited many other non-profit organizations.

In 1960 Governor Bill Egan signed a bill leasing PARCA forty acres of land in perpetuity. That land, on Northern Lights Boulevard east of Goose Lake, is The ARC's current home. State government showed its support again in 1961 when Governor Egan signed a law mandating special education for mentally retarded children throughout the state.

Meanwhile, PARCA's school thrived. After three years in Quonset huts, the school moved to Trinity United Presbyterian Church in Spenard. The ASD paid rent for the space and paid the teachers' salary.

Construction of the new building proceeded at a steady pace. The work was made possible through donations of time and equipment from the community and nearby military installations. Construction had to be postponed in 1964 when the Good Friday Earthquake rocked the city and made reconstruction Anchorage's first priority. Also in 1964, the organization changed its name from PARCA to Association for Retarded

Children of Anchorage (ARCA) reflecting the entire community's involvement in the success of the organization.

In November 1968 the brand new ARCA building was ready to open its doors. The building was totally financed with private funds. Bob Reeve, founder of Reeve Aleutian Airways, was chairman of the building drive. Leo Frelin and Frank Wince, local engineers, donated their services as project directors, and Modern Construction Company was the builder.

ARCA continued to press the ASD to provide "free and appropriate" public education. As a result of this persistence and cooperation from the ASD, Anchorage developed one of the first special education programs in the country that provided regular school programs for every child, regardless of severity or complexity of disability.

In 1969 ARCA leased five acres of its property to Hope Cottages, where the fledgling organization built its first residence facility for babies with mental retardation.

ARCA was becoming more aware of the need for programs for adults at the same time that a group of local vocational training professional developed a "sheltered workshop" located in the Spenard area. The two groups decided to work together. ARCA assumed ownership of Chugach Rehabilitation, Inc. in 1971, and the center operated from federal Vocational Rehabilitation Agency funds and from performance contracts with private and public agencies. The workshop employed a large staff and included a variety of persons qualified to receive workshop training. There was a period when all Anchorage telephones were repaired and renovated there, and most utility bills were mailed from the workshop! Soon the makeshift facility in Spenard wasn't adequate, and plans for a new building were formulated. In 1975 Anchorage attorney Frank Smith spent many hours with ARCA committee members planning a new building. Seattle architect Arnold Gagnes provided superior architectural service at no cost to ARCA. The program moved into its new building on Northern Lights Boulevard in 1976.

This workshop thrived for two years, but as the population increased and demands became higher, fiscal problems emerged. In

1979 Rehabilitation Industries, Inc. was forced to declare bankruptcy and the State of Alaska assumed proprietorship. Fortunately, the takeover was accomplished without impeding the program, and the non-profit agency was continued with a new board of directors and incorporation. The agency is known today as ASSETS and provides many services to the community.

The Special Olympics, an extremely positive and successful athletic program established for those experiencing disabilities, was established in Anchorage in 1971. ARCA families supported and participated in Special Olympics enthusiastically, to the great benefit of everyone involved.

The special education facility, the Helen S. Whaley Center for Learner Assistance opened in 1973. Its well-timed opening coincided with a law passed by the Alaska Legislature requiring public schools provide preschool education beginning at age three for children with determined special needs.

As ARCA grew and needed to hire paid employees, a predictable income was necessary. This need resulted in ARCA's entrance into the thrift and gift shop business. The first shop opened in 1970 was between Eighth and Ninth Avenues and K and L Streets downtown and was called the "Thrift and Gift Cache." This shop was the beginning of what is now

ARC of Anchorage preschoolers, c. 1970.

Value Village on Northern Lights Boulevard. The ARC provides clothing and merchandise to TVI, Inc., which manages the store.

In 1979 the original preschool was expanded by 15,000 square feet and in 1989, ARCA began operating an Activity Center to provide drop-in social and learning programs to adults with disabilities. That facility expanded in 1984 to include a kitchen, multi-purpose room, barrier-free bathrooms, gymnasium and office space. It was renamed the Arctic Resource Center in 1990 and continues to operate.

ARCA then looked into offering help to the families of those benefiting from its programs. A system was developed for providing respite services, giving parents much needed time when their special child would be cared for by a trained adult so that parents could enjoy some time away. This was the beginning of a broad array of services to families.

The services ARCA provided eventually became the "rights" of individuals experiencing disabilities and were increasingly funded by state, federal, and local governments. More staff was hired to carry out the services and volunteer activity declined substantially, following a pattern nationwide.

In 1979 ARCA membership decided to begin a daily activity program to provide social opportunities for young adults who were placed in the sheltered workshop. After their four or five hour shift, workers could walk up the short path from the workshop to the building at 2211 ARCA Drive and enjoy activities with friends. The Activity Center has included courses in cooking, arts and crafts, communication skills, and reading, and provides group activities in the community such as "dinner out and a movie," concerts and other Anchorage activities.

The first group home provided by The ARC was ready for occupancy in 1985. Through the application process to select eight residents for ARCA House, it became apparent that there was a great need for more housing. Within a short time two more homes

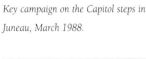

Key campaign on the Capitol steps in Juneau, March 1988.

near DeBarr Road were purchased to accommodate four persons each. This program became so popular and the demand so high that by the year 2000, just fifteen years later, The ARC had developed twenty-eight homes.

In response to the requests of many families, ARCA became a partner with the ASD in providing summer enrichment programs in 1985. Although the school district is no longer involved, ARCA continues to provide an individualized enrichment program for over fifty school age children, always in inclusive settings where average children can have the opportunity to be friends with children who experience disabilities.

In 1987 The Foundation of The ARC was created. The purpose of the Foundation is to both provide a Special Needs Trust program for families of persons who experience disabilities and to develop a substantial corpus of private funds available to enhance services already in place. The Foundation exists solely to provide for the same population as that of The ARC of Anchorage.

The "Alaska Youth Initiative," a program serving severely emotionally disturbed children and adolescents in appropriate residential settings were begun in 1986. Some time later, ARCA was encouraged to provide services to "dually diagnosed" people, who experience developmental disabilities and mental illness. The decision to accept persons who qualified broadened ARCA's base as a service provider considerably, and enlarged the circle of professional agencies and service providers with whom ARC interacts on a regular basis.

In 1997 ARCA's name was changed to The ARC of Anchorage. Also in 1997, another wing was added to the existing building to make room for The ARC's expanding workforce.

The most recently begun services include the Substance Abuse Program and the Deaf and Hard of Hearing Center. The Substance Abuse Program is a residential treatment program for persons who can benefit from substance abuse treatment, and are persons who are eligible for services from The ARC. This is a new field and a real challenge for professionals. The Deaf and Hard of Hearing Center joined The ARC's cadre of programs in July 1999.

The history of The ARC of Anchorage reveals an incredible story of hundreds of determined individuals making monumental efforts to enhance the lives of special Alaskans so that everyone can truly optimize their personal potential. It is still an organization with one purpose—to serve those who experience disabilities. It exists for people, about people, and by people.

❖

Past ARC of Anchorage presidents (from left to right): Bob Mothershead, Terry Ribilyn, Karen Ward, Margaret Lowe, Kathy Fitzgerald, and John Burns, October 1997.

ANCHORAGE CHRYSLER DODGE

The Anchorage Fur Rondy World Championship Sled Dog Races hadn't been televised in years. In 1999 Rod Udd, president of Anchorage Chrysler Dodge Center (ACD), called the television station to find out why. He was told it was due to lack of sponsorship. "Well, I could do something about that," he said. That's how Anchorage Chrysler Dodge became an official sponsor of the Anchorage Fur Rondy Sled Dog Races. "And to make it fun for the mushers, I put up a Dodge Durango for the winner."

Involvement in the community is one of the things in which Udd is most proud about his company. "We are a local, Alaska-owned corporation," he explains. "And we don't have to send money to investors in the Lower Forty-eight, so we can contribute to our local communities and activities of interest to the Alaska people."

Udd started working as a salesman in 1973 and became president in August 1989 when he purchased the company. In his years at ACD, it has enjoyed continual steady growth. ACD's business increased during the pipeline, as it did for other local businesses, and moderated somewhat after. Business has been growing steadily ever since. ACD currently enjoys revenue of $64 million per year.

Many early Anchorage businesses started in humble metal buildings. In 1963 ACD became one of those. The company was first located on Fifth Avenue, just west of today's Dodge

Building. ACD has grown to outperform all Chrysler Dodge dealers in Alaska and rank second in the Pacific Northwest. In 1999 *Alaska Business Monthly* magazine named ACD sixteenth in business in Alaska when ranking its 1999 "Top '49ers." This distinction singles out Alaskan owned and operated companies which stand out above their peers as the most successful for-profit businesses based on 1998 gross revenues.

Kenneth B. Davis and Glen Phillips started this ultra-successful dealership in 1963 as Fifth Avenue Chrysler. (In 1965, Phillips sold out to Davis, making him the sole owner of the dealership.) Anchorage was a city of over ninety thousand at that time, and it was already establishing itself as a headquarters for the Alaskan oil industry. By the early 1960s, eighteen oil companies had already opened offices in Anchorage, and geological survey crews were beginning to operate in Alaska. The future looked bright for ACD, as it stood ready to serve the employees and families of these companies flocking to the community.

In no time ACD needed more room than their little metal building could offer, so a new structure was built at 2501 East Fifth Avenue. The business sold cars there right up to the Good Friday earthquake on March 24, 1964. When the quake struck at 5:36 p.m., employees huddled under their desks waiting for the shaking to stop. They watched as the quake, originally rated 8.4 on the Richter scale but subsequently upgraded to 9.2, caused the glass portion of the building to collapse on top of the showroom's shiny new automobiles. Amazingly, though, no one was hurt. Although it was a difficult time for the staff, ACD wasted no time rebuilding, and the new store, a sturdier concrete building, opened in February 1965. The company operated in this facility until October 9, 1972, when the Chrysler Building was completed. At this time, Chrysler Plymouth was moved to the new building and Dodge opened next door at 2501 East Fifth Avenue.

In November 1969, Chrysler Corporation became a partner with Davis, and the name was changed to Anchorage Chrysler Center, Inc. Marketing Investment Division (MID), doing business as Chrysler Motors Corporation operated the business with Davis until December 1978 when Davis retired. By this time, facilities had expanded vastly to include many services.

In April 1979, Ray Sutton and Joseph Leavitt, Sr., came to Alaska from California to see the growing facility. They agreed that it was an interesting investment. They soon moved their families to Anchorage and set to work. Anchorage Chrysler Center, Inc., under the direction of these strong leaders, became one of the highest-ranking Dealers in the United States. ACD has received many awards from the factory, such as qualifying for membership in the Charger Club and the Pace Makers Club. Some employees have enjoyed awards and trips due to exemplary dealership standing.

Since the new Chrysler Building opened in 1972, the dealership has expanded to cover 4.5 contiguous blocks on East Fifth Avenue. The location, says Udd, is excellent, as commuters drive by on their way to work and again on their way home in the evening. Should a customer want to stop to check out a new Dodge Ram pickup, Chrysler mini-van or even a Hummer, Udd has a staff of 140 people who are happy to assist. Staff at ACD point to the Dodge Ram pickup (as evidenced by the rows of pickups on display along Fifth Avenue) and Chrysler mini-vans (customers love the cup holders!) as the most

popular items. Currently, a new PT Cruiser decorates the dealership's front lot. ACD took so many orders for the new automobile on its first day at the dealership (forty-eight) that the factory called to ask them to stop taking orders, as ACD was selling them too quickly! Despite the dealership's already high visibility, Udd still hopes to achieve a higher profile image on Fifth Avenue in the future, and thinks that perhaps one day ACD may expand to other locations in and around Anchorage.

One look at area parking lots or a drive down any Anchorage street will illustrate just

✧

Interior and exterior views of Anchorage Chrysler Dodge's location on Fifth Avenue.

what kind of popularity ACD already enjoys. Dodge Ram pickups, Neons, Chrysler Town and Country and Dodge Caravan mini-vans seem to be everywhere. Commuters will also see the occasional Hummer, especially during the long, slippery winter driving months.

Fans of the Iditarod are especially excited when they spot the Official Iditarod Dodge Ram pickup on the road. That means the driver is a winner of the Iditarod, like Jeff King, three time winner, or Doug Swingley, three-time winner and record holder.

These pickups have been donated primarily by ACD since 1990. Alaska Dodge dealers, in particular ACD, have helped the Iditarod committee immensely by sustaining sponsorship in a time when many corporations have backed out of race sponsorship due to political pressure. The Iditarod would no doubt be in jeopardy should local businesses like ACD not support the event. ACD enjoys great visibility at the ceremonial start of the race that takes place in downtown Anchorage. Although the majority of mushers are still from Alaska, participants, tourists and journalists from around the world get a close look at the Iditarod winner's first prize Dodge Ram pickup.

ACD also recently helped to recognize an Iditarod hero. Joe Redington, Sr., known in Alaska as the "Father of the Iditarod," worked tirelessly in the race's early years to see that it became a reality. Shortly after moving to Alaska in 1948, Redington bought a team of dogs, established Knik Kennels and, in his spare time, brushed out portions of the historic Iditarod Trail. He also lobbied successfully to have it added to the National Historic Trails System. Redington, Sr., was a frequent participant in the race until his death from cancer in 1999. His death was a great loss to Alaskans, especially sled dog racing fans. In recognition of his efforts, Udd sponsored development of a Joe Redington, Sr. bronze memorial trophy, which was unveiled in Nome, Alaska, at the finish of the 2000 Iditarod.

Visibility has also increased by ACD's introduction into the world of cyber sales! Because of the remote areas in which many Alaskan shoppers live, the Internet is the perfect way for ACD to reach its customers. The web pages, www.alaskacarnet.com and www.alaskatrucknet.com, feature information on everything a shopper could need: the Chrysler, Dodge, and Plymouth automobiles, Hummers, sales and lease options, incentives, information on service and parts, employment, pre-owned vehicles and commercial fleet sales. It even offers links to other interesting Alaska websites.

The Iditarod and the Anchorage Fur Rendezvous are not the only way ACD stays involved in community activities. Udd himself is on the Board of Directors of the Boys and Girls Clubs of Anchorage and the Intervention Helpline. ACD sponsors many charity golf tournaments, Cook Inlet Soroptomist events and Habitat for Humanity projects. Udd is very proud of ACD's sponsor-

ship in local amateur car racing events. "The idea," he explains, "is 'hey, kids, don't race on the streets, do it at the track.'" The walls of his office are covered with thank you photos and plaques from the many charities ACD has helped throughout the years.

The City of Anchorage has grown and matured in the thirty-seven years since ACD first opened its Quonset hut doors on Fifth Avenue. The population of Anchorage in 1963 was 93,685——by 1996 it had grown to 254,269, comprising almost forty-two percent of Alaska's total population. Slow, steady growth has replaced the earlier boom and bust economies and a steadily increasing population has filled empty homes and offices built during the oil boom in the 1980s. While Anchorage continues to be the center of Alaskan oil business activity, tourism has begun to take hold as Alaska's most promising source of future revenue.

Through the years, the products ACD has been able to offer have expanded. No one in 1963 had ever heard of a mini-van, and certainly no one had driven a Hummer down the street! ACD has been able to provide the newest and best products to the Anchorage community. With continued community involvement, ACD will no doubt carry on its reputation as a leader in the Anchorage business world.

Rod Udd was honored by receiving the "2001 Quality Dealer Award" from *TIME* magazine.

✧

Above: Three-time Iditarod winner Doug Swingley receives the keys for his prize, a Dodge Ram pickup, from Rod Udd.

Below: Rod Udd, owner of Anchorage Chrysler Dodge presents the October 2000 "Anchorage Chrysler Dodge Anchorage Aces Player of the Month" trophy to Paul Williams. Williams is a member of the Aces, the local semi-pro hockey team.

ALASKA HOUSING FINANCE CORPORATION

Alaska Housing Finance Corporation was originally developed to help families find homes after World War II. It has evolved into an organization that now contributes more than $100 million annually to Alaska's state revenues through cash transfers, capital projects and debt-service payments.

Alaska's population increased from about 4,000 in 1940 to 9,000 just one year later. But when the war ended, families left by the hundreds—not because of a lack of employment, but because of a severe shortage of housing. To that end, the Alaska Territorial Legislature created the Alaska Housing Authority (AHA). When the Federal Housing Act of 1949 was passed, it authorized the federal government to make up to $1.5 billion in loans and grants nationwide for slum clearance and redevelopment. AHA was appointed the agency to work with Alaska in urban renewal.

AHA fulfilled these roles until the 1959 Alaska Statehood Act, when AHA became known as the Alaska State Housing Authority (ASHA). Throughout the 1960s, ASHA was the key source of housing, including affordable rental and homeownership programs, bonding for government office space, and urban renewal, especially following the devastation of the 1964 earthquake.

In 1971 the Alaska Legislature created the Alaska Housing Finance Corporation, a public corporation having legal existence independent of and separate from the State of Alaska to

provide affordable housing for low- and moderate-income residents. During AHFC's first two years of operation, the ten-member staff provided nearly $10 million in conventional mortgages in forty communities and financed a ninety-eight-unit apartment building in Juneau. In 1972 the Legislature created the Department of Community & Regional Affairs, repealing ASHA's community planning authority and transferring those duties to DCRA.

For the next twenty years, AHFC, ASHA, and DCRA each provided housing services to a distinct segment of Alaska's population. Products included programs for a state mortgage insurance program, rehabilitation loan programs, and rural and mobile home mortgage programs. In 1992 the Legislature recognized a need for all of the state's housing programs to come together, precipitating a merger of AHFC, ASHA, and the housing and energy programs of DCRA. Today, AHFC's Public Housing Division continues the role that AHA began fifty years ago, while the Research and Rural Development Division has assumed the duties previously administered by DCRA.

AHFC is the only housing authority in the United States with true statewide jurisdiction. The challenge of size and remoteness in Alaska, along with its extreme climate, demands innovative solutions that have become models

Above: The home of the Ward family in Haines, Alaska.

Below: Dormitories for the University of Alaska Anchorage.

for other housing authorities and housing finance agencies nationwide. Alaska's population of 620,000 is spread across an area one-fifth the size of the entire United States (Alaska is two and a half times the size of Texas!). From the tip of the Southeast Panhandle to the furthermost island in Alaska's Aleutian Islands spans a distance equaling that from California to Florida. The majority of Alaska is accessible only by air.

Throughout its more than fifty years, AHFC has provided assistance to thousands of Alaskans in more than two hundred often-remote communities. While best known for financing single-family homes, its diverse programs include community planning and development, direct and pass-through grants, technical assistance, tax credits, affordable rental housing, energy/weatherization programs, drug-elimination programs, computer learning centers, breakfast for children, programs to coordinate services, self-sufficiency programs, and youth sports activities.

Through targeted programs, AHFC can have direct, positive impact on the community. For instance, in June 1996 the Miller's Reach fire devastated the Wasilla/Big Lake communities sixty miles north of Anchorage. More than 37,500 acres burned, destroying 344 buildings valued at $8.8 million. AHFC's emergency loan program provided gap financing and initial

construction funds while fire victims awaited insurance settlements, private construction-loan financing or federal/state emergency assistance funds. Made available through AHFC's arbitrage funds, the loans provided zero interest for two years, then 3.875% interest for up to 13 years. During this crisis, AHFC took 86 applications and closed 42 loans for a total of $1.05 million. AHFC received a national HUD award for its response to the crisis.

AHFC continues to make its most tangible impact on the Alaskan homebuyer through innovation. In 1999 AHFC provided financing under the tax-exempt program for 2,182 first-time homebuyers, bringing total homes financed under that program to 15,446 for $1.3 billion. In August 2000 AHFC introduced a new loan program to reach a broader group of Alaskans by offering first-time homebuyer loans that do not restrict the purchase price or the income of the borrower.

AHFC has been recognized with numerous national awards, such as the annual Award for Significant Achievement from the National Council of State Housing Agencies, Award of Merit from the National Association of Housing & Redevelopment Officials, and one hundred percent on HUD's Public Housing Management Assessment Program four consecutive years.

A key to AHFC's success is its strong credit rating. AHFC's ability to issue highly rated taxable and tax-exempt bonds helps keep mortgages affordable and provides Alaska with the financial means to fund capital projects.

❖

Above: Chugach Manor Senior Housing, Anchorage, Alaska.

Below: Bethel home ownership program, Bethel, Alaska.

BP IN ALASKA

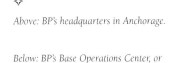

✧

Above: BP's headquarters in Anchorage.

Below: BP's Base Operations Center, or BOC, at Prudhoe Bay.

BP is responsible for oil and gas exploration, development and production in Alaska, and provides oversight of the company's interests in the Trans Alaska pipeline and pipelines from producing fields on the North Slope—Kuparuk, Milne Point, Endicott, and Badami. Beginning in 2001, it will operate the pipeline from its newest offshore field, Northstar.

BP is one of the world's three largest integrated energy companies. It has about 100,000 employees and operations in 100 countries on six continents. BP is the largest natural gas producer and distributor in North America.

BP was among the first companies to explore Alaska in the late 1950s, and actively participated in lease sales in the 1960s to develop a strong position in the Prudhoe Bay area on Alaska's North Slope.

Following the Prudhoe Bay field discovery in 1968, BP quickly began development on its leases. The first oil flowed from North America's largest oil field on June 20, 1977.

Over field life BP has invested more than $9 billion for production operations, facility expansions, drilling and oil recovery programs, many of which required advances in technology.

BP has invested another $7 billion in oil fields that were later brought on stream, including the Kuparuk, 1981; Lisburne, 1986; Endicott, 1987; Pt. McIntyre and Niakuk, 1994. In 1994, BP acquired the Milne Point field, to the west of Prudhoe Bay, and in 1998 started producing the Badami field, about thirty-five miles east of Prudhoe Bay. Other smaller fields in which BP has an interest are Midnight Sun, West Sak, Tabasco, Tarn, Eider, and Sag Delta North.

BP has been a leader in technology, pioneering new drilling and oil recovery techniques that have helped yield significantly greater volumes of oil than anticipated when fields were first discovered. For example, the Prudhoe field was initially believed to contain about 9.6 billion barrels of recoverable oil. In 1999, the ten-billion-barrel mark was passed. By using modern drilling

the company holding an interest in more than nine trillion cubic feet (TCF) of the North Slope's approximately thirty-five TCF. The company's goal is a major gas sale from Alaska before the end of the decade and it is working with other companies to explore all options for commercializing this vast resource.

During its forty years in Alaska, BP has set high standards in environmental protection and stewardship. Through advances in directional drilling and improvements in drilling waste disposal, the company has significantly reduced the amount of land impacted by oil and gas development. Restricting construction to the winter months when the ground is frozen has also reduced surface impacts. Extensive environmental monitoring programs focused on air and water quality, tundra vegetation, fish, birds, and marine and terrestrial mammals have shown that impacts from North Slope oil field development have been minimal.

BP has played an active role in communities across the state in its support of education, social services, civic organizations, arts, youth sports and environmental programs. Its employees are encouraged to be active volunteers in their communities.

The company has led efforts to train and hire Alaskans and to purchase supplies and materials from Alaska-based vendors. A new Alaska-based industry, oil field module fabrication and construction, is a primary example.

BP looks forward to a long and rewarding future as a leading corporate citizen and a major producer of North Slope oil and gas.

techniques and oil recovery programs it is believed that another three billion barrels will be produced.

Today, BP has an interest in fifteen North Slope oil fields, and is a major holder of North Slope oil and gas reserves. The company operates nine of those fields, including Prudhoe Bay. Combined, the fields produce more than 800,000 barrels per day—about eighty percent of North Slope oil production.

BP is one of Alaska's largest oil producers and corporate taxpayers, part of an industry that provides an average of about eighty percent of the state's annual revenues. Through taxes and royalties on North Slope oil production, BP has been a primary contributor to the state's Permanent Fund, valued at about $27 billion in 2000, which each year provides a dividend to each Alaska resident.

Early in 2000, the U.S. Federal Trade Commission approved BP's merger with Atlantic Richfield, contingent upon the sale of ARCO's Alaska assets to Phillips Petroleum, Inc., BP, Phillips and Exxon Mobil subsequently realigned ownership at Prudhoe Bay and established BP as the sole operator of the Prudhoe Bay field.

The realignment also strengthened BP's natural gas position on the North Slope—with

❖

Above: BP-contracted drilling rig on Alaska's North Slope.

Below: BP's Northstar project was about half complete in May 2000 and was expected to begin producing oil in 2001.

SPENARD BUILDERS SUPPLY

❖

Top, right: The original Spenard Builders Supply store at Minnesota and Tudor Roads in Anchorage as it looked in the late 1950s before it was destroyed by fire.

Above: Ed Waite, president of Spenard Builders Supply.

Opposite, top: Spenard Builders Supply flagship store at Minnesota and Tudor Roads.

Opposite, middle: The interior of a Spenard Builders Supply store.

Opposite, below: With three distribution centers, Spenard Builders Supply has the ability to buy and stock building materials in volume.

You wouldn't know it now, but when Spenard Builders Supply first opened its doors at the intersection of Tudor and Minnesota, the store was out in the "boondocks." In 1952 those roads were both bumpy, unpaved dirt trails. The founders, George A. Lagerquist and A. J. Johnson, chose this out of-the-way location because of its easy access to the Alaska Railroad lines. This spot also offered plenty of room to grow—something that SBS has done a lot of since opening!

Originally only three employees served customers at the Spenard location. In 2000 SBS employed more than 600 persons and operated 11 retail locations, 3 distribution centers, 2 truss plants, and 3 millwork facilities throughout the State of Alaska. In 1952 the primary products sold were lumber and plywood. Today, SBS customers—both contractors and do-it-yourselfers—depend on the truss plant, millwork shop, countertop shop, professional paint center, and design center showroom.

Growth and adaptability have been the keys to SBS's success through the years. In the latter 1950s and early 1960s, the people at SBS were kept very busy trying to keep up with the building boom in both the public and private sectors of the community. In particular, the military was expanding in south-central and interior Alaska, and the state's population was growing accordingly. SBS was able to expand to accommodate its customers, meeting their demand for quality building supplies.

That ability to serve customers became critical to the city's survival after the Good Friday Earthquake of March 24, 1964. Although the earthquake did extensive damage to the SBS facilities, the company was open for business the next morning to help Alaskans cope with the excruciating task of rebuilding. After reconstructing its own facilities, SBS set its sights higher and expanded into Alaska through catalog sales and a network of salespeople statewide. To ensure up-to-the-minute communications with its sales force, the company installed a Teletype, which was then the ultimate in communication technology in Alaska.

Just three years later SBS was hit hard by another disaster. Fire destroyed everything at the Spenard location, including warehouses and inventory. Once again the determined people at SBS managed to open for business the following morning in two small salvaged cabins. Instead of weakening the company, these disasters seemed to galvanize the firm and make it stronger and even more determined to succeed. SBS finished the year of 1967 with $2 million in sales and constructed its largest building materials complex in the state at the same location.

The firm began to expand rapidly in 1976, when it opened its first branch store in Wasilla, followed two years later by the acquisition of Alaska Builders Supply in Fairbanks. In 1978 the firm decided to call all of the branch stores Spenard Builders Supply. That year also marked the merger of SBS with the Lanoga

Corporation of Redmond, Washington, owner of United Building Centers, with stores from Wisconsin to Montana and Lumbermen's Building Centers, based in the Northwest.

In 1979 the company erected GALCO Building Products, Inc., a distribution warehouse for its stores, located on the Old Seward Highway in Anchorage. That same year, SBS acquired Baranof Building Supply in Sitka. Establishment of a purchasing office in Seattle in 1980 helped place SBS in the mainstream of the building commodities market, ensuring its customers the continuity of product lines and consistent low prices. Also in the 1980s, SBS acquired stores in Kenai, Soldotna, Homer, Kodiak, and Glenallen, broadening its services to Alaskans.

The middle years of the 1980s were tough for Alaska, as oil prices fell, construction ground to a halt, banks failed and thousands of homes were left empty as their owners left the state. The population of Anchorage dropped from a high of 240,000 in 1985 to a low of 219,000 in 1988 before beginning to recover.

The 1990s saw slow and steady growth as the Alaskan economy diversified. Retail, tourism, mining, and fishing have all played a part in this stabilization. SBS expanded in the 1990s to Barrow, on the Arctic Ocean, and Seward, on the Kenai Peninsula. SBS has eleven yards as well as three distribution centers, two in Anchorage, and one in Tacoma, Washington.

Although growth is very important to SBS, it is also important to management that it remains a good place to work. The company's philosophy has been not only to make SBS profitable, but also to make it a good place to work. It would seem that they are successful in that quest, as forty percent of its six hundred employees have been with the company for more than ten years.

And, of course, good old-fashioned customer service is the backbone of SBS. They believe firmly that the customer ultimately decides the fate of their business, and strives to achieve constant improvement towards customer service. In fact, their talent for recognizing and being responsive to their customers changing needs is what keeps Alaskans coming back to SBS, making them the leader in building products in Alaska.

CSX Lines

On April 24, 1964, the largest earthquake in North American history blasted through South-central Alaska. The damage was enormous. Badly needed relief supplies began moving toward Alaska by air, water and highway. Once the situation stabilized, the quantity of supplies that would be needed to rebuild the state became staggering.

Unknown to most Alaskans, the first company that successfully commercialized freight containerization on a large scale, Sea-Land Service, Inc., was already planning to inaugurate the first regularly scheduled weekly-containerized freight service between the Pacific Northwest and Anchorage. The service was to start in the Fall of 1964. When Sea-Land officials learned of the huge quake, they scrapped the Fall plans and redeployed vessels to begin the new Alaska Service immediately. The first

Sea-Land Alaska containership, the *S.S. New Orleans*, arrived in Anchorage from Seattle on May 7, 1964 laden with 1,640 tons of cargo.

To this day, CSX Lines, the former Sea-Land, continues the maritime tradition begun that day in May 1964: safe, reliable, professional containerized ocean service from the Pacific Northwest to Anchorage and back every week of the year.

Longtime Alaskans well remember the name of Milt Odom. Odom built a statewide distributorship of consumer products over many years in the mid-twentieth century. In order to support his growing concerns in the 1960s, Odom purchased Alaska Freight Lines (AFL) from Lloyd Burgess in 1961. Odom's purchase of AFL ensured that his businesses would have a steady reliable supply of goods from the Lower 48 at rate levels Odom could control. Malcolm McLean, Sea-Land's founder, purchased AFL from Odom in October 1963.

Years earlier, Malcolm McLean had introduced containerization to America's East Coast when he founded Sea-Land. At that time he was not aware that a small ocean freight company, started by Alaska businessman Al Ghezzi, was already utilizing containers to move freight on their own barges between Seattle and Valdez, Alaska. Ghezzi's company, Alaska Freight Lines, was the same company that McLean would buy years later from Milt Odom.

The ocean transportation of goods to Anchorage involves unique challenges. The greatest tidal forces of any commercial port in the world combined with the harsh Alaskan winters create a difficult and dangerous journey for the crew and cargo. CSX Lines' three 710-

foot containerships, *CSX Anchorage, CSX Kodiak,* and *CSX Tacoma,* were built in Sturgeon Bay, Wisconsin specifically for use in Alaskan waters. Ice banded hulls, non-contiguous fuel tanks, bow and stern thrusters, variable pitch propellers, 22,540-horsepower diesel engines, and advanced electronic navigation aids all contribute to ensuring CSX liners transit the Cook Inlet and the Gulf of Alaska safely every time.

CSX Lines sails twice a week from Tacoma to Anchorage, twice a week from Anchorage to Kodiak and once a week to Dutch Harbor. They also serve communities in the Aleutian and Pribilof Islands and Bristol Bay with seasonal feeder barge service. CSX Lines is the largest shipping company in Alaska, having shipped over one and one-half million containers to Alaska since 1964.

A wide range of equipment is available from the company to meet any shipping need including dry, open-top, refrigerated or insulated containers, flatbeds, and car carriers. The vessels carry such goods, as automobiles, electronics, sporting goods, construction equipment and the household belongings of those moving to and from Alaska.

CSX Lines Freight Service handles transport inland from Anchorage. Their drivers deliver goods anywhere the roads go. When the roads end, CSX Lines continues operating via connecting carrier services on barges and aircraft. CSX Lines Freight Service has some of the finest truck drivers in the State of Alaska. Many have been with the company since the days when the Trans-Alaskan oil pipeline was constructed.

CSX Lines' Alaska headquarters is in Anchorage. They have a strong commitment to the state and contribute to many organizations. Some of these include the Boys and Girls Clubs, The Salvation Army, Special Olympics, United Way, Anchorage Concert Association, State and local Chambers of Commerce, Junior Achievement, and the World Championship Junior Sled Dog Races. CSX Lines also supports the Alaska SeaLife Center in Seward, the Providence Hospital renovations in Anchorage, the new health clinic in Dutch Harbor and numerous sports teams.

✧

Above: A pilot guides the CSX Tacoma *into Dutch Harbor.*

Below: Working at the Port of Dutch Harbor.

AT&T
ALASCOM

AT&T Alascom is the only communications company in Alaska that has been in the state since the beginning—since 1900, to be exact. In a state that spans 367 million acres and five varied regions, telecommunications on the last frontier takes on an even greater importance. Over the past hundred years, Alaskans have come to regard AT&T Alascom as a way of life.

What is now AT&T Alascom began as the Washington-Alaska Military cable and Telegraph System (WAMCATS) in 1900 when Congress passed an act ordering communication channels to open between Alaska's isolated military outposts and the rest of the United States. That year, under the leadership of Billy Mitchell, the first operational telegraph link was completed, with twenty-five miles of line strung from Nome military headquarters to the Port Safety outpost.

By 1905, 3,607 miles of landlines, submarine cable, and wireless links comprised the unique and growing network. Provided that traffic didn't interfere with their operations, the military allowed commercial and non-military entities to utilize the system. Eleven years later half of the current WAMCATS lines were abandoned in favor of new wireless stations, reducing costs and increasing reliability.

During the 1930s submarine cables slowly replaced the talking wire. To reflect the changing technology, Congress renamed WAMCATS the Alaska Communications System in 1936. The system forged ahead, especially in the 1940s when the war effort increased the need for dependable communications.

In the mid-1950s, thirty-five years before making Alaska its permanent home, AT&T laid a new submarine cable between Ketchikan and Port Angeles, Washington, resulting in upgraded communication between Alaska and the lower forty-eight states.

Meanwhile, RCA Global Communications had won contracts to supply personnel and maintenance to scattered Armed Forces communication sites in the state, and as they became more involved in Alaska communications, the federal government decided to stop providing communications to the commercial and private sectors. In 1969 the United States Congress passed the Alaska Communications Disposal Act and put the current military owned system up for bid. RCA was the successful bidder and the unified company was soon known as Alascom.

In 1972 new technology brought direct distance dialing to the last frontier, and by the late 1970s Alascom had expanded its service in Alaska by constructing more than 200 earth stations and serving even the smallest rural communities in the state.

Company pride and commitment to Alaska was never more evident than on October 27, 1982, when Alascom launched its own satellite, *Aurora I*, the only satellite of its kind dedicated to one single state. Live television, which was a given anywhere else in the United States, was just arriving in Alaska. No longer would Alaskans have to wait a week, or

sometimes two, for favorite entertainment programs and sporting events.

Along with the launch of *Aurora I*, Alascom's plant improvements had vastly upgraded its satellite and terrestrial links within the state and to interstate points. A new multi-purpose building was constructed on Government Hill, consolidating the company's components in one complex.

On May 29, 1992, Alascom launched its second satellite, *Aurora II*, replacing the aging *Aurora I* after nine faithful years of service. The new satellite continued to provide a variety of telecommunications services to the growing population of Alaska. Alascom also entered the age of fiber optics by linking its network with the North Pacific Cable that runs from Oregon to Japan, a length of 5,200 miles.

Two strong heritages were merged on August 5, 1995, when telephone giant AT&T purchased Alascom. AT&T's rich history dates back to 1876 when Alexander Graham Bell and Tom Watson were testing an idea for a telephone in Boston, and Alascom's history began twenty-four years later in 1900 with Captain Billy Mitchell and WAMCATS. What we have today is a company with two tremendous histories offering telecommunications services to virtually every Alaskan community.

AT&T Alascom currently employs about 500 people statewide and handles in excess of 95 million calls per year. AT&T has spent over $200 million in capital improvements in Alaska in the past five years, and successfully launched its third satellite, *Aurora III*, on December 19, 2000, reinforcing its commitment to the last frontier. This determination to deliver service to all Alaskans has resulted in one of the largest satellite networks for telephone service in the world.

Bringing people closer together—it's the greatest benefit of AT&T Alascom's technology and community service. In conjunction with AT&T's philanthropic efforts, the company actively participates in the AT&T CARES program. AT&T CARES allows every AT&T employee to devote one paid workday per year to volunteer at a non-profit organization of his or her choice. This commitment is valued at approximately $20 million nationally. AT&T Alascom associates have donated thousands of hours to communities throughout the State of Alaska.

The rich heritage that began with Alexander Graham Bell and Billy Mitchell continues today at AT&T Alascom—Alaskans working to bring all Alaska within reach of the world.

✧

Above: AT&T Alascom Headquarters, Government Hill, Anchorage, Alaska.

Below: AT&T Alascom Earth Station, Minchumina, Alaska.

CRAIG TAYLOR EQUIPMENT

When Craig Taylor first came to Anchorage, he didn't have much capital. But he recognized a land of opportunity when he arrived in 1953. Today his company does a thriving business throughout Alaska.

The Taylors moved to Alaska from Boise, Idaho, via Whitehorse, Yukon Territory. Whitehorse was too small for Taylor's dreams —the sternwheeler still brought provisions to the town—and the young family continued northward. When they stopped in Anchorage, it was a growing town enjoying post-war prosperity and a construction boom.

Taylor quickly took a job with Northern Commercial selling heavy equipment at its downtown Anchorage branch at Fifth Avenue and H Street (currently home of the Glacier Brewhouse). The family lived in an apartment on the second floor of the Northern Commercial General Store at Fourth Avenue and H Street (now a parking lot). His job was a step in the right direction, but Taylor had bigger plans.

Until the late 1950s the John Deere product line had always been sold with Caterpillar equipment. The companies split that year, and Craig saw this as his big opportunity. He borrowed money from his mother-in-law, Hazel May, to attend the Association Equipment Dealers convention in Chicago. He was able to convince the John Deere Industrial Company that he was the man to represent their line in Anchorage. Craig Taylor Equipment (CTE) was born!

The first CTE welcomed customers in a store on the corner of Concrete and Commercial Avenue on property Taylor leased from Art Waldron, owner of Anchorage Sand and Gravel. They moved when the property they currently occupy became available in 1956. Craig Taylor Equipment now has stores in Fairbanks, Soldotna and Wasilla. They carry many lines–John Deere Lawn & Garden tractors and mowers, Bobcat loaders, Dynapac compactors, Kobelco excavators, Lister Petter engines, Echo chainsaws and garden equipment, and Vermeer equipment. They even sell those sturdy John Deere toy tractors for kids and collectors.

Above: Craig Taylor, 1984.

Below: Craig Taylor Equipment, 1960.

CTE has played a significant role in the history of Alaska. The company was ten years old and Anchorage was suffering from an economic slowdown when North America's most devastating earthquake rocked Anchorage. The quake set off landslides in three of the most built-up areas of the city. The Fourth Avenue downtown business area was devastated, while the "L" Street and Turnagain slides practically leveled Anchorage's most populated areas. Mrs. Taylor had front row seats to the devastation in the Turnagain neighborhood, as she watched it through the windows of her living room. Houses right across the street were totally destroyed, while the Taylors' residence was spared. Anchorage didn't have time to feel sorry for itself, though, and the town was soon engrossed in a massive clean-up and rebuilding effort. Individuals and developers alike turned to CTE for help with equipment to rebuild the city.

Just a few years after the Anchorage earthquake, in 1968, a flood washed over Fairbanks and the city was immobilized. Craig Taylor was told that he couldn't go to Fairbanks because the city was flooded, but in characteristic style he went anyway. He hired a helicopter to lower him onto one of the John Deere tractors on the lot at his Fairbanks branch. Taylor pulled the ever-present keys out of his pocket, started up the tractor and drove through town pulling people to safety.

The discovery of oil on the North Slope and the business generated by the pipeline made a major change in the company. CTE was enjoying a business of about $1 million per year when, seemingly overnight, it increased to $2 million per month. The company now enjoys steady growth.

Craig Taylor died on November 18, 1987, leaving the business to his son Mike and wife, Thelma. "It started out as a family business and it still is," says Mike. "I like it that way." CTE currently employs sixty-five people. "It's not so big I can't know everybody," he says. CTE is one of the few Alaska family owned corporations still in business. "All the family businesses used to work together," he remembers. "We still do."

The Taylor family now spends a good deal of the year at their horse ranch outside of San Diego, California, at the foot of Tecate Mountain.

The walls of Mike's office are decorated with racing photos of some of their winning thoroughbreds, ridden by the likes of jockey legends Gary Stevens and Eddie Delahoussaye. Like their equipment business, the ranch is a family operation. Mike and his wife, Maureen "Marty" Taylor and his mother live there, and aunts live nearby. Mike makes sure he is in Alaska during the busy summer business months, and enjoys fishing on the Kenai.

The story of Craig Taylor and his equipment company is very much an Alaskan story of opportunity. CTE wants its customers throughout Alaska to know that, while many companies come and go, CTE was here to help build Alaska before the pipeline and plans to serve Alaskans well after.

✧

Above: As Alaska continues to grow, environmental improvement and economic development should complement each other to ensure healthy, vibrant communities. CTE's quality growth philosophy is the foundation for successful business; it will be promoted throughout our next fifty years in serving Alaska's equipment requirements.

Below: Although the Anchorage location is the same depicted in the 1960 photograph on the facing page, the equipment technology is keeping up with the pace of change Anchorage has gone through over the half century Craig Taylor Equipment has been serving Alaskans.

KETCHUM AIR SERVICE, INC.

"Ketch" Ketchum's Alaskan flying career started in 1967 flying seismic equipment in a single-engine Otter to the North Slope. Today Ketchum Air Service, Inc. (KAS) is best known for flying thousands of adventurers to some of Alaska's most beautiful and remote spots, providing the experience of a lifetime to whomever answers their invitation: "C'mon, let's go fishing!"

Ketchum's aviation career started long before his arrival in Alaska. He flew with the Army Air Corps during World War II in almost every type of aircraft available to the military, from the AT-6 to the B-36, including transports on C-46s in the South Pacific theatre. When the war was over, Ketchum flew with a domestic commercial airline flying coast to coast in DC-3s.

Ketchum's early commercial piloting career was cut short by escalation of the Cold War in Germany. His family moved to the U.S. air base at Wiesbaden, Germany, where he flew in the Berlin Airlift. Ketchum stayed in the military after the airlift, moving his family every year until an assignment of four years in England. Ketchum's son Craig, age six at the time, remembers his father taking a bowler hat and "brolly" (umbrella) before setting off to work in London's Whitehall district, the center of British government. Their next move to Shreveport, Louisiana, happened just before the United State's involvement in the Vietnam conflict. He was offered a commission to Vietnam, but chose early retirement.

In the spring of 1965 the Ketchums traded their Shreveport household for an Airstream trailer and headed toward California. Upon reaching California the Ketchums kept going until pulling up in Anchorage, Alaska, on a dark, drizzly August day. The small community was busy rebuilding itself just a few months after the Good Friday Earthquake. Plenty of jobs were available for people willing to work hard, and Ketchum quickly found a job in the construction business.

The family—Ketch, wife Marguerite, and children Steve, Craig, and Nancy—liked Anchorage's small town atmosphere. The children enjoyed the schools and made new friends. The town's casual attitude also appealed to them. One New Years' Eve, Ketchum spent the day working on a tarpaper roof. Remembering the holiday, he stopped at the new Hotel Captain Cook to make celebration reservations for himself and his wife. Upon returning home he discovered his face was covered with tar. It occurred to him that the hotel concierge had treated him professionally and respectfully, regardless of his appearance. It was at that moment Ketchum decided Anchorage was home.

In 1967 Ketchum made another revelation—he didn't like construction but he loved to fly. He started working for Ward Gay, a well-known Alaskan aviator, flying seismic equipment to the North Slope and fishermen to remote places in the summer. Although he loved flying, Ketchum's demanding work schedule created stress on the family. In an attempt to change that, he purchased Jim's Flying Service, came up with the slogan "Let's Go Fishing to the Real

Alaska!" and started flying customers from the shores of Lake Hood to outlying camps.

KAS was, and still is, a family business. In the beginning, Marguerite ran the business while Ketch flew and the kids helped out where they could. Their son, Craig Ketchum, partner and current manager of KAS, became involved as a teenager helping with odd jobs. Craig received a degree in mechanical engineering from the University of Washington in 1972. He came back to Anchorage, started working at KAS full-time, and married his high school sweetheart, Bertsie. Craig and Bertsie now own and operate KAS. Although Ketch and Marguerite are officially retired, they are still busy promoting the business by handing out brochures wherever travels in their new Airstream RV may take them.

The Ketchums have always been looking for ways to expand the business to meet the needs of customers. One such opportunity knocked in March 1989 in Prince William Sound when the *Exxon Valdez* ran aground. Upon hearing the news, Craig flew to Valdez where KAS eventually had five airplanes serving the area. It was the most dramatic change in the history of the business, and KAS still flies for clients involved in the incident.

Home base for KAS is on the shores of Anchorage's Lake Hood. They also fly customers from bases in Valdez and Cordova. KAS has forty-two fishing and hunting cabins in

remote Alaska and several houseboats in Prince William Sound. KAS has ten floatplanes and flies over 12,000 clients per year. The company offers an exciting diversity of products to suit customers' desires, from guided fishing trips to secluded houseboat excursions. Some customers have been coming back to fly with them for thirty years!

The Ketchums believe their staff can provide an experience that cannot be duplicated anywhere in the world. They want their customers to be completely enamored of Alaska. When people get back to Anchorage with a gleam in their eye, the Ketchums and their staff know they have done their job.

Above: Marguerite and "Ketch" Ketchum, 1967.

Below: Ketch, Marguerite, Craig, and Bertsie Ketchum, 1998.

HICKEL INVESTMENT COMPANY

When Walter J. Hickel's train arrived in Anchorage in November 1940 he had only thirty-seven cents in his pocket. Today Hickel is chairman of the board of Hickel Investment Company, which has real estate, hotel, shopping centers, and other assets throughout Alaska. Although his business accomplishments are impressive, somewhere between his arrival and the year 2000 he found time to be governor of Alaska twice, serve as secretary of the Department of the Interior during the Nixon administration, and establish an Arctic-wide association of twenty-three Arctic regions called the Northern Forum.

Hickel grew up in Kansas, the oldest son of ten children. "We weren't poor," he says, "we just had no money. There's a big difference!" He wanted to be a boxer, so he set out for California in 1940. When he saw the Pacific Ocean he thought about going on to Australia, but because he didn't have a visa, he chose the next farthest place—Alaska. "California seemed like the end of the world," he remembers. "Alaska, the end of the earth." Six days north of Seattle he saw the Wrangell Mountains in the sunlight and "pretty near" got homesick. He looked up and said, "If you take care of me, I'll take care of you."

Upon arrival in Alaska, however, Hickel was too busy to be homesick. "I wanted to work for myself," he says. "I started out as a civilian inspector on the Army Air Force Base,

Above: Hotel Captain Cook, Fourth Avenue and "K" Street, Anchorage, Alaska.

Below: Walter and Ermalee Hickel, c. 1995.

and kept on going, always looking to solve problems." The Hickel Investment mission statement is "Building a Better Alaska," and Hickel started his business by doing just that. He watched as people left Anchorage in droves after World War II, not because there wasn't work or they weren't happy here, but because there wasn't enough housing. "People were living in tarpaper shacks," he remembers. "There were very few places available to live." In 1946 he started building houses and in 1947 Hickel Construction was formed. In two years' time his new company had built 100 units and had started renting them.

In 1951 the Hickel Company, Inc. was founded. A string of development projects followed. In 1953 the Traveler's Inn of Anchorage was built, and the Traveler's Inn of Fairbanks was built two years later. In 1956 Hickel joined J. C. "Muktuk" Marston in developing the Turnagain-by-the-Sea area. Hickel brought the newest in shopping concepts to Alaska in 1959 when the state's first shopping center, the Northern Lights Shopping Center, was built. In 1958 the Hickel Investment Company became incorporated. A few years later, it completed and opened the Mountain View Shopping Center.

As with many business people of Anchorage, Hickel's future was radically affected by the Good Friday Earthquake on March 27, 1964. Many business leaders were taken aback when Hickel announced plans to build a luxury hotel downtown. The

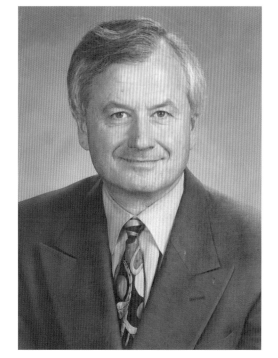

Hotel Captain Cook opened Tower One on July 17, 1965, and has prospered ever since. Subsequent towers were built in 1972 and 1978. Hickel Investment Company opened the University Center of Anchorage in 1972 and in 1977 opened a similar complex, the University Center of Fairbanks.

Hickel Investment purchased the Fifth Avenue Office building in downtown Anchorage in 1984. That same year, expansion on the University Center of Anchorage was begun, and Hickel Investment started development of Resolution Pointe. On July 19-21, 1985, the company enjoyed the grand opening of the Valley River Shopping Center in Eagle River. Other properties currently owned by Hickel Investment include Eastside Storage, Central Storage, and the "Little White House," a historic, early Anchorage house at 935 West Third Avenue.

Hickel Investment Company is a property ownership, development, and management company employing 450 persons. Hickel is chairman of the board and his son, Robert J. Hickel, is president.

In addition to his business career, Hickel served as governor of Alaska in 1966-69 and 1990-94 and secretary of the Department of the Interior in 1969-70 during the Nixon Administration. He also has a long history of public service on a local level: he served as the founding director of the Providence Hospital Health Care Foundation from 1983 to 1990; the Providence Hospital Advisory Board, 1975 to 1988; the board of trustees at Alaska Pacific University from 1959 to 1991; and served as a member of the board of directors of Boys Club of Alaska from 1969 to 1974 and Trustee from 1981 to 1984. He was elected a lifetime honorary member of the Boys and Girls Clubs of Greater Anchorage Foundation Trustees, May 29, 1996. Hickel was a major donor to the Alaska SeaLife Center, and the Hickel Investment Company was a major contributor to the new Alaska Native Heritage Center.

With a seed gift of $1 million to Alaska Pacific University, as well as large in-kind support, Hickel has founded the Institute of the North to study management of common resources, Arctic and Alaska strategy, and to serve as a home for the Northern Forum, a non-governmental organization of regions around the North.

Hickel and his wife, Ermalee, live in Anchorage. They have 6 sons and 16 grandchildren and enjoy travel in Alaska. "There is so much to see in Alaska," he says. "This is great country. It's unique geographically, geologically, people wise, climate wise." Hickel's philosophy is simple. "You have to have ideas. If you have ideas and belief, the money will come along."

✧

Left: Robert J. Hickel, president, Hickel Investment Company.
COURTESY OF BOYER PHOTOGRAPHY.

Right: Walter J. Hickel, Jr., president, Hotel Captain Cook.
COURTESY OF BOYER PHOTOGRAPHY.

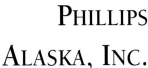

PHILLIPS ALASKA, INC.

Alaska's history would look much different without the impact the oil industry has made on the state. Since Phillips' first exploration near Cordova in 1952, their legacy spans nearly five decades. Throughout the years Phillips Alaska and its heritage companies, Phillips Petroleum and ARCO Alaska, have been key players in one of the brightest chapters in Alaska's history book. The pages of the book are filled with the people and events that have shaped the Alaska we know today. What a different picture it would be without Phillips' contributions to the state. Those contributions include not only oil discoveries, but also the building of the Trans Alaska Pipeline, co-funding the Alaska Permanent Fund and millions in community contributions.

And to think it all started with a little luck. In 1952 Phillips Petroleum Company was the first to receive permission to drill in Alaska. Other companies followed, but the initial results included 165 dry wells. In 1956 it was ARCO's test well at the Swanson River that discovered oil. Ultimately that discovery helped convince Congress that Alaska was worthy of statehood.

Luck was with the company again in 1968 when a last chance well, drilled by ARCO (now Phillips Alaska) and Humble Oil Company (now Exxon), discovered America's largest oil field–Prudhoe Bay. The discovery resulted in $900 million worth of lease bonus payments to

Above: The Phillips Alaska building is headquartered in Anchorage.

Below: The Central Arctic Caribou herd migrates to the North Slope oil fields each summer for calving.

the state and began an oil boom that changed the state's economic landscape for good.

Later that year, ARCO, BP and Exxon formed the Trans Alaska Pipeline System (TAPS), which Phillips and three other companies joined to begin what was the largest civil construction project ever undertaken—an eight-hundred-mile pipeline from Prudhoe Bay to Valdez.

Environmental concerns and Native land claims delayed the building process for nearly six years; however, the secretary of the interior approved construction in 1973. Construction of the $8-billion pipeline began in 1974. In June 1977 the first oil was shipped through the pipeline.

In 1968 Phillips began operating the Kenai LNG Plant, which manufactures liquefied natural gas (LNG). The plant was the first large-scale commercial export of LNG from the United States to Japan.

By the late 1970s oil was on its way to replacing the military as the backbone of Alaska's economy. Pipeline construction changed the last frontier forever. The state became home to new, experienced laborers, the education level of Alaska's population improved and salaries increased, as did the price of real estate.

The 1980s were challenging times for the state and the industry as oil prices hit new

lows. However, all-time record low prices didn't materialize until 1998, when sub-$9 per barrel oil brought on major consolidations within the industry. BP announced the purchase of ARCO, an event that transformed the face of the Alaska oil industry and gave birth to Alaska's newest oil company— Phillips Alaska.

As part of the merger, Phillips Petroleum Company acquired the stock of ARCO Alaska, Inc. This new company is also one of the oldest because the men and women of Phillips Alaska share the proud Alaska heritage of two great companies, Phillips Petroleum and ARCO Alaska. In 2001 Phillips Alaska will celebrate forty-nine years of pride and history in the forty-ninth state.

Our legacy includes the discovery and development of the largest oil fields in Alaska: the Swanson River in 1952, Prudhoe Bay in 1968, Kuparuk in 1981, Point McIntyre in 1989, Alpine in 1994 and the Meltwater field in 2000.

It's a legacy that has set the standard for success and responsible development, a standard that Phillips Alaska is proud to continue.

In late 2000 the men and women of Phillips Alaska completed yet another chapter in Phillips history with the start-up of the Alpine oil field. This 429-million-barrel oil field has set a new standard for minimal impact on the environment and responsible development. The forty-thousand-acre field was developed using just two-tenths of one percent of the surface area. It's also helped to set new standards for Alaska buy, hire, and build.

Phillips Alaska is proud of its past and excited about the future. Yes, they have some big shoes to fill, but what better way to make their forefathers proud than to do it bigger and better. Phillips Alaska is the state's largest producer of Alaska North Slope crude oil and gas, the largest state and federal leaseholder, and far and away the state's most aggressive explorer.

Phillips Alaska has nearly 900 employees in Alaska and another 350 maritime employees working for its shipping unit, Polar Tankers. Its operations include Kuparuk, Alpine, and the Kenai LNG Plant. Phillips holds major ownership in Prudhoe Bay, Kuparuk, Alpine, Point McIntyre and nearby satellite oil fields. In addition, Phillips Alaska holds ownership interest in more than eight trillion cubic feet of North Slope natural gas.

✧

Above: The Alpine oil development sits on just ninety-seven acres, using two-tenths of one percent of the field's surface area.

NATIONAL BANK OF ALASKA

President Harding in Anchorage July 17 1923

Perched on the brink of merging with Wells Fargo, the mood at National Bank of Alaska (NBA) is one of optimism for the future and pride in the past. Although some things will certainly change as a result of the merger which took place in 2000, the Bank's commitment to the State of Alaska will not. After a quick review of NBA's history, the upcoming merger can be seen as one in a series of events that have helped build Alaska's largest banking institution.

NBA began as the Bank of Alaska and first opened its doors in the gold rush town of Skagway, Alaska in March 1916. Andrew Stevenson, the bank's first president, thought Alaska was the right place for a modern system of banks and invested $50,000 in capital to make it a reality. Stevenson didn't waste any time proving his point—by early May of the same year a branch opened in Wrangell, and a few weeks later one opened in a fledgling "tent city" on the shores of Cook Inlet, later to be named Anchorage. Business entrepreneurs and city leaders Z. J. Loussac, J. B. Gottstein, and Sydney Lawrence were among its first depositors.

The Bank of Alaska had just begun to establish itself when World War I brought financial hardship to Alaska. E. A. Rasmuson, the bank's attorney, was appointed as temporary president in 1918, a post officially assigned him a year later, thus beginning the family's colorful leadership at NBA. By 1920 the state's economy, especially that of Anchorage, was flagging. Anchorage had enjoyed a strong economy based on the building of the Alaska Railroad, but World War I and the influenza epidemic of 1919 caused an end to that. Anchorage's population, estimated at 6,000 in 1916, dropped to fewer than 2,000 in 1920. In spite of the slowdown, the Bank of Alaska reported deposits exceeding $1 million.

Rasmuson, upon visiting United States President Warren G. Harding in 1922, invited him to visit Alaska—NBA's Skagway and Anchorage branches in particular. Harding and his wife came in 1923, making him the first president of the United States to visit Alaska. In July 1922, Harding drove the "golden spike," completing the Alaska Railroad.

While the World War I caused economic hardship, World War II brought unprecedented

growth and development to Alaska. The military chose Anchorage as its construction hub, and its population more than doubled from about 4,000 in 1940 to 9,000 a year and a half later. With this influx of military personnel, the Anchorage Bank of Alaska branch deposits exceeded $4 million almost overnight.

In 1943 Rasmuson was appointed the Bank of Alaska chairman of the board after serving as its president for twenty-four years. His son, Elmer, was elected president. The growing city of Anchorage became the bank's official headquarters in 1946 and its Fourth Avenue and "E" Street location downtown became its flagship branch. Soon after, in 1949, E.A. Rasmuson died of a heart attack at the age of sixty-six. He died just before the Bank of Alaska became the National Bank of Alaska (NBA) by charter of the federal government.

Elmer Rasmuson appealed to the Alaska legislature to allow branch banking. In 1951 legislation was passed to allow it within a 100-mile radius of bank headquarters. When Alaska attained statehood in 1959, the bill was repealed, enabling even more growth. In 1964 the third generation of Rasmusons joined the bank when Edward became assistant cashier of the Ketchikan branch.

The Anchorage economy had leveled off by 1964, when the Good Friday Earthquake rocked the city, killing 115 people and causing heavy damage to property. NBA's International Airport branch was completely destroyed, and other branches were damaged. NBA assisted in the reconstruction of Anchorage by processing hundreds of loans. Elmer Rasmuson was soon elected mayor of Anchorage after campaigning on the need for a long-range plan for reconstruction of Anchorage after the earthquake and beyond.

NBA celebrated its fiftieth anniversary in 1966 as the largest bank in Alaska with 280 employees and deposits exceeding $100 million. NBA outgrew its downtown Anchorage headquarters and moved to the corner of "C" Street and Northern Lights Boulevard in 1977. NBA brought the electronic age of banking to Alaska in 1982 by installing automated teller machines (ATMs) in five locations. By its seventy-fifth anniversary in 1991, NBA had $2 billion in assets and 53 branch locations in 29 Alaska communities and Seattle.

When seeking an avenue into the Alaska market, Wells Fargo looked for a well-run, solid company and found it in NBA. Currently, Edward Rasmuson, chairman of the board, and Richard Strutz, president of NBA, lead the state's largest bank, with more than $3 billion in assets and a network of 54 branches, 150 ATMs, and 4 community agents. They will continue to do so after the merger with Wells Fargo.

And so, after eighty-four years of service, National Bank of Alaska is turning over a new leaf. Alaskans, however, can expect the same commitment and community involvement from the bank. For instance, in the past several years, the bank has committed over $1 million annually to nonprofit and community organizations. Also, NBA's Heritage Library and Museum established in 1968 in the bank's headquarters will continue to operate. And the products and customer services Alaskans have come to know and rely upon will still be just around the corner.

✧

Above: The Anchorage branch of Bank of Alaska, 1916.
COURTESY OF THE ANCHORAGE MUSEUM OF HISTORY AND ART, NO. B80.194.1.

Below: A 1953 photo of the National Bank of Alaska headquarters on 4th Avenue and E Street in Anchorage.
COURTESY OF THE ANCHORAGE MUSEUM OF HISTORY AND ART, WARD WELLS STOCK NO. 1452.2.

ALASKA SALES AND SERVICE

In a town with many transient residents, it is not surprising that car dealerships come and go in Anchorage. But Alaska Sales and Service (AS&S) has been here since 1944 and are determined to be strong well into its next fifty-six years. They depend on repeat customers and referrals for business and strive to provide superior products and services at competitive prices to earn the trust of those customers.

AS&S has flourished under the leadership of strong businessmen throughout the years. Founder Max B. Kirkpatrick and four associates first started AS&S in 1944. Kirkpatrick's was the story of an enterprising individual seizing opportunity when it occurred. He moved from Kansas to Cordova, Alaska, in the late 1930s to work as an aircraft mechanic for his brother, an Alaskan bush pilot. He subsequently invented coal-mining machinery, and worked in the airline, television, and tug and barge businesses before coming to Anchorage and founding the dealership.

In 1949, James D. Medema joined Alaska Oil Sales & Service, Inc., an associated corporation of AS&S from 1945 to 1962. Medema became part owner in both companies in 1956. Max D. Hodel, a partner in AS&S, joined him. A. Douglas Hulen joined Alaska Oil Sales &

Service, Inc. in January 1958 and moved to AS&S when the oil sales company was sold. Hulen served as vice president and general manager for several years before becoming part owner in the firm in 1973. Hulen served as president from July 1986 to July 1991 at which time Leonard Bryant became president/dealer.

From its very beginning, AS&S has sold General Motors products. AS&S originally held the franchises for Chevrolet, Oldsmobile, Pontiac, Cadillac and GMC Trucks. A Buick franchise was added in 1975. In 1952, AS&S expanded their customer services by forming Alaska General Credit Corporation, a wholly owned subsidiary providing financing and insurance products. AS&S is Alaska's only full line General Motors dealership.

In 1944, AS&S occupied temporary facilities in downtown Anchorage while the building on Third Avenue and "E" Street, across from the Hilton, was constructed. When AS&S outgrew that location, it purchased land on East Fifth Avenue near Merrill Field, previously home base of Alaskan bush pilot Hakkon Christensen. Construction began in 1963, but Mother Nature had surprises in store. The Good Friday Earthquake in 1964 destroyed eighty percent of the building. No one was hurt because the building was still under construction, but large sections of the roof and walls collapsed. Rebuilding took some time—the new AS&S headquarters wasn't completed until February 1965. When it opened, the new 40,000-square-foot facility was the talk of the town. It seemed an overwhelming size for a city of just over 100,000 people, but AS&S had an eye toward the future of Alaska and its many opportunities for growth.

In 1969, facilities expanded even further to include a body shop building, a heavy-duty truck shop in 1974, and used car and truck sales facilities. The dealership also expanded into the daily car rental business by affiliating a licensee of National Car Rental in 1968, with main offices located on Third Avenue and five outlets in Homer, Kenai, Seward, Wasilla, and Valdez. A new operations center was built in 1972 at the Anchorage International Airport for the convenience of arriving visitors.

AS&S currently employs 265 people and is consistently listed among the top ten Alaska-owned businesses by the *Alaska Business Monthly*.

Leonard Bryant, current president, started at AS&S in 1965 as a mechanic and has stayed because he enjoys the challenge. Through his years there, he has been exposed to almost every job in the company. "There was opportunity here," he remembers, "there still is. Alaska Sales & Service offers a broad foundation for people." He believes AS&S's success is due to their commitment to the customer. "The relationship with the customer is the most important thing. Without that you don't have any success," he says. "We try not to sell to a customer once, but for their entire lifetime, and that of their family and neighbors. We do the job in a way that will make the buyer think of us next time he needs a car. Sixty percent of our business is from repeat customers."

Bryant is also proud of the fact that AS&S is an Alaskan owned business and that it is involved in many community activities. He especially likes to see the business become involved in activities which interest AS&S employees, like United Way and Boys' and Girls' Clubs.

Bryant is well aware of the reputations of many car dealerships. "Alaska Sales and Service has been in business a long time, because of the loyal customer base. If people take the time to get to know us, they'll find we're different. Honesty and integrity is important to us. We're very concerned with our image."

✦

Alaska Sales and Service located at 1300 East 5th Avenue.

PERATROVICH, NOTTINGHAM & DRAGE, INC.

✧

Oil field module construction at the Port of Anchorage required an "Open-Cell" dock for module transfer to ocean-going barges. As of the year 2000, over ninety "Open-Cell" structures have been built for many different purposes.

PHOTO BY ROB STAPLETON. COURTESY OF VECO ALASKA.

Peratrovich and Nottingham, Inc. was formed in 1979, a time when many businesses called it quits due to the economic downturn caused by the beginning of the end of the oil boom. The firm later changed its name to Peratrovich, Nottingham & Drage, Inc. (PN&D). The company's founders, civil engineers Roy Peratrovich, Jr. (University of Washington), Dennis Nottingham (Montana State), and Paul Reynolds (Notre Dame) were determined to ride out the slow economy. If they provided the best product possible through excellence in engineering for the lowest possible cost, they would succeed. Indeed, their objective carried them not only through the tough times of the early 1980s, but into today's prosperity.

Before establishing their company, the three worked together on a variety of projects. Their combined engineering background included over 200 bridges and many maritime facilities and civil engineering projects. They also contributed significantly to large, award-winning projects such as the 300-mile Parks Highway and the world renowned Trans-Alaska Pipeline.

Their goal was to provide superior engineering by assembling a highly experienced staff located in key geographical areas. Quality control was paramount. Applied engineering would be emphasized in the disciplines of geotechnical, marine, bridge, and arctic engineering, and engineering principles would be supplemented by extensive research. The engineering professionals would prepare professional papers for national and international dissemination, and would deliver in-depth presentations on technical subjects.

The firm has followed its original objectives very closely. Thirty of the firm's sixty employees are registered engineers. PN&D believes in the "lattice" management structure, pointing out that most companies have fewer registered engineers than technicians, compromising the quality of their product. PN&D's customers know a quality professional is in charge of their project. PN&D has emphasized slow and steady growth because its leaders did not want to expand beyond their capacity.

Currently, about sixty percent of PN&D's business is marine related and includes ports and harbors from the far north to California and the East Coast. They've designed many bridges on Alaska's North Slope and their "Module Bridge" over the Kuparuk River, the world's strongest bridge, has won national awards.

Although the company started in Alaska, they now get business from all over the world. Clients in other locations were reluctant to employ an engineering firm in Alaska, claiming their circumstances were different. But more and more, that attitude is changing, and PN&D has projects underway in Maine, Louisiana, Illinois, Florida, Oregon, California, and Russia.

A snowstorm in Seattle several years ago was a turning point for PN&D's involvement in out-of-state projects. Many of Seattle's covered marinas collapsed under the weight of the unusually heavy Christmas snowfall, and agencies turned to PN&D for help. Suddenly, the Alaskans' design expertise was in high demand. Their "Open Cell" innovation, in particular, brings calls in from places like Ireland, Japan, South America, Russia and the "Lower 48." There are currently ninety-four "Open Cell" bulkhead structures worldwide.

PN&D has strong Alaskan ties. Roy Peratrovich, Jr., is the first Alaskan Native to be a registered engineer. He is the son of Roy and Elizabeth Peratrovich, native Tlingits and Alaskan civil rights leaders. In 1945, the Peratroviches lobbied the Territorial Legislature to enact anti-discrimination laws, enabling all citizens of Alaska, including Alaskan Natives, the privileges of citizenship without discrimination. Mrs. Peratrovich is highly credited with being the persuading voice during the hearings. Roy Peratrovich, Jr., recently donated his mother's collection of memorabilia, documents and papers to the Smithsonian Institution's National Museum of the American Indian. PN&D also contributes to community activities such as the United Way and many charities.

Dennis Nottingham does his part to ensure that projects in Alaska will continue to improve and meet expectations by teaching part of an arctic engineering course at the University of Alaska–Anchorage. Construction projects in the north are rife with challenges, and he volunteers the benefits of his research and experience to help others understand Alaska.

Paul Reynolds, a running back for Notre Dame's National Championship football team and an experienced engineer and contractor met an untimely death shortly after PN&D was formed. Brent Drage, a later owner, also died suddenly. These men contributed to PN&D's early success, and both Paul & Brent are remembered daily with a great sense of loss.

Many of PN&D's projects have won awards for innovative design. The West Dock Causeway, the Endicott Causeway on the North Slope, the Tudor Trail Crossing in Anchorage, and the Port of Seattle Bell Street Pier Wave Barrier are a few examples of PN&D's insistence on excellence in engineering. Other state-of-the-art projects include Seward's Deep-Draft Coal Port, the fifty-four-mile-long Red Dog Mine Access, and Saint George Harbor, including a new $17 million, rubble-mounded berm breakwater (designed to withstand fifty-foot offshore waves in the Bering Sea). These projects supplemented the already extensive experience of founding members, which encompassed nationally significant projects such as the first cable-stayed bridge in the United States located in Sitka, Alaska; the Hurricane Gulch Bridge, one of the longest-span arch bridges in the country; and various bridges along the Trans-Alaska Pipeline route, such as the award-winning, half-mile-long Yukon River Orthotropic Pipeline/Highway Bridge.

✧

Top: The Tudor Trail Bridge has won many Local and National awards, and has been featured Internationally as a most beautiful bridge.

Above: Racing sled dogs use the Tudor Trail Bridge.

ARECA, ALASKA'S ELECTRIC ASSOCIATION

ARECA, Alaska's Electric Association, is the trade organization for electric utilities in Alaska. It provides advocacy and program services to help its thirty-seven active and contributing members in their efforts to serve consumers with affordable, reliable electricity and to improve the quality of life in Alaska's communities. ARECA also offers members the opportunity to participate in the ARECA Insurance Exchange. It was created in 1952 by Alaskan electric cooperatives—but its story actually begins in the 1930s!

The Great Depression wreaked havoc in American families from coast to coast. Two federal programs designed to alleviate the devastation came together to help create rural electric associations in Alaska. President Franklin Delano Roosevelt signed the Rural Electrification Administration (REA) order in 1935, potentially transforming the lives of rural residents throughout the country, including the Territory of Alaska. The REA was designed to provide low-interest loans to those communities willing to take on the challenge of building electric systems and paying back loans.

Meanwhile, over two hundred colonists had arrived in the undeveloped Matanuska Valley—later known as Palmer—in May 1935 to begin new lives after drought destroyed their Midwest farms. They asked the REA for help in organizing a cooperative in 1937, and in 1940 were authorized to form the Matanuska Electric Association (MEA), Alaska's first electric association. In spite of the onslaught of World War II, MEA worked diligently to build a transmission line to tap the power of a small hydroelectric plant in the Eklutna area. Supplies

were hard to come by, but, in spite of their difficulties, MEA began distributing electricity to 127 members in April 1942.

As Alaska grew, many Alaskans turned to cooperatives to meet their electricity needs. MEA service was extended to Chugiak in 1944. People living outside the city limits of Anchorage, Fairbanks and Juneau formed their own cooperatives when local utilities could not meet their demand. In 1947 Fairbanks consumers created the Golden Valley Electric Association, which was soon serving 129 customers in North Fairbanks and the surrounding area. Residents of Auke Bay, near Juneau, formed the Glacier Highway Electric Association in 1947. The Chugach Electric Association was also formed in 1947 when two hundred people met in the Anchorage High School Auditorium to create

what would become the state's largest electric utility. In 1950 Chugach had 2,136 customers—by the end of the decade they had 12,500.

By 1952 six electric cooperatives served areas in or around Anchorage, Fairbanks, Homer, Juneau, Kodiak, and Palmer. This group formed ARECA to share information and promote rural electrification. The timing for such an organization could not have been better, as demand for electricity grew statewide by leaps and bounds in the coming years.

In the 1970s, Alaska's electric utilities were faced with the challenge of dramatically increasing electric needs when construction of the Trans-Alaska Pipeline began in 1974. Once again, Alaska's electric cooperatives were called upon to work together to solve the crisis created by high demand, rising fuel costs and increased labor costs and shortages.

In recent years, population growth and escalation in technology has necessitated ARECA's involvement in helping to meet the demands of consumers. One of the biggest problems facing Alaska is the high cost of electricity in rural Alaska—almost four times the cost in Anchorage! The Power Cost Equalization (PCE) program was developed to help minimize that disparity. In 2000 ARECA successfully lobbied two bills signed by Governor Tony Knowles allowing divestiture of the Four Dam Pool hydroelectric facilities in Southeast Alaska to their respective communities, and establishing a PCE Endowment for long-term PCE funding.

Today, ARECA members provide power to more than 556,000 Alaskans throughout the state. The technical, physical and political setting in which Alaska utilities provide their service is very different from that of the rest of the North American continent. Alaska does not have the vast infrastructure of transmission interties that provide so well throughout the rest of the United States, nor for the biggest majority of the state, are its communities and towns served by even a rudimentary road system. Alaska also differs from the rest of the country in that a majority of its residents are served by rural electric cooperatives.

Nevertheless, ARECA members have established solutions and operating procedures to overcome these daily obstacles. Currently, Alaska utilities are experimenting with distributed generation including fuel cells, wind power, hydropower, computer-enhanced systems and micro turbines with much success.

ARECA could not exist without the dedication of hundreds of individuals who have served their communities through their rural electric associations. As long as Alaskans need electricity, ARECA, with its Anchorage-based staff and statewide board of directors, will be here to help keep Alaska's future bright.

PHILLIPS' CRUISES & TOURS

Brad and Helen Phillips pioneered the day cruise industry in Alaska. They started Phillips' Cruises & Tours in 1987, bringing years of experience in tourism and navigation to Alaska's Prince William Sound. That experience, combined with their enthusiasm and love of Alaska, has helped make their "26 Glacier Cruise" a must-do for thousands of tourists and residents every summer.

Brad Phillips' career in the tourism industry began shortly after his service with the U.S. Army Air Corps during World War II. He started working as a sightseeing driver and guide in Fairbanks, Alaska in 1948. In 1958 he was the first to realize the potential in tourism in Prince William Sound and started taking passengers on "Columbia Glacier Cruises," originating in Valdez. After just six years, the devastating 1964 earthquake and resulting tsunami washed their boat out to sea —the *M/V Gypsy* was never seen again. The company he and his wife, Helen, formed, Prince William Sound Navigation Company, Inc., replaced the Gypsy with the *M/V Glacier Queen*, which sailed between Valdez and Whittier. Phillips continued to work in many facets of the Alaska tourism industry while making time to earn a BBA from the University of Alaska and University of Miami, a Masters from Cornell University and Juris Doctorate from the California Western School of Law.

Helen Phillips, co-owner and executive vice president of Phillips Cruises and Tours, has extensive experience in the travel industry. She has owned and operated two travel agencies, written training manuals, and conducted training sessions for travel industry sales and service personnel for Westours Alaska, and in 1972, she and Brad formed the Prince William Sound Navigation Company, Inc. In 1982, the Phillips formed Yukon River Cruises, Inc., and built the M/V Klondike, a seventy-six-foot Catamaran passenger vessel (the first of its kind in the United States), and operated tours between Dawson City, Yukon Territory, and Eagle, Alaska during the 1985-1986 seasons.

In 1987, doing business as Phillips Cruises and Tours, they moved the *M/V Klondike* into Prince William Sound and began operating the "26 Glacier Cruise" from the Port of Whittier. Phillips Cruises and Tours strives to provide Alaska's premier one-day cruising experience,

sending every visitor to Alaska home absolutely convinced that their one-day cruise adventure with them was the highlight of their Alaskan visit. Today's passengers enjoy the beautiful scenery of Prince William Sound in a new state of the art 420 passenger, 38 knot, K Class Catamaran, *M/V Klondike Express II*. This vessel affords unobstructed viewing inside and three viewing decks outside—Prince William Sound does the rest! The "26 Glacier Cruise" provides views of 135 miles of glaciers, marine wildlife and the most breathtaking scenery in Alaska. The cruise departs from Whittier, Alaska, and travels through Port Wells to College and Harriman Fjords, cruising in close, safe proximity to massive tidal, piedmont and alpine glaciers that date back hundreds of thousands of years. Passengers find that Prince William Sound's protective waters create the perfect habitat for countless species of marine wildlife and sea birds that fly from all over the world to nest during the summer months. Orca and Humpback whales are commonly seen, as well as sea otters and seals lounging on ice flows, bear's roaming the low lands and mountain goats climbing the steep slopes that border the tidewater glaciers.

Phillips Cruises and Tours have their headquarters in Anchorage and a seasonal sales office in Whittier. The company employs 11 persons year-round, 10 of whom are based in Anchorage, and adds approximately 22 additional employees during the operational season.

Both Brad and Helen are very involved in the community. Helen is currently president of the Anchorage Chapter of Altrusa International and served on the Alaska Tourist Advisory Board, an appointment made by Governor Walter J. Hickel

in 1969. She serves as a board member for the National Association of Cruise Only Agencies and the Anchorage Convention and Visitors Bureau. She is also involved in the Alaska Visitors Association, the Prince William Sound Tourism Coalition, the National Tour Association, Cruise Lines International Association and Travel Industry Association of America.

Brad served the community in political venues, as well as civic. He served on the Anchorage City Council during 1956-1960, two years of which he was mayor pro tem. He was chairman of the President's Civil Rights Advisory Commission for Alaska (an appointment made by President Dwight D. Eisenhower). From 1960-1970 was a member of the Alaska State Senate, serving as president, majority leader, minority leader, chairman of the Legislative Council, vice chairman of Legislative Council, chairman of Rules Committee, and served on the Finance, Labor and Management, State Affairs, Local Government, and Legislative Audit Committees. His civic duties include director of the Anchorage Chamber of Commerce, Alaska State Chamber of Commerce, and Anchorage JAYCEES; board member of the Alaska Visitors Association, Anchorage Economic Advisory Council, and Providence Hospital Advisory Board; member of the Alaska State Bar, and fund drive chairman for the American Cancer Society, March of Dimes, Alaska Heart Fund, Armed Forces YMCA, Alaska Crippled Children's Association, and the United Fund.

✧

Above: Visitors enjoying the view aboard the M/V Klondike Express II.

Below: Typical wildlife seen on Phillips' Cruises and Tours.

ALASKA USA FEDERAL CREDIT UNION

Anchorage was enjoying a post-war boom when the Alaska USA Federal Credit Union (Alaska USA) was chartered at Fort Richardson, Alaska in 1948. The credit union's fifteen founding members felt that local financial institutions were not adequately meeting the needs of federal civil service personnel who had recently transferred to Alaska. Today, Alaska USA is Alaska's largest consumer financial institution, the state's primary provider of consumer credit, and a leader in developing electronic financial service options. The credit union is a not-for-profit cooperative, serving over 220,000 members worldwide.

After the credit union was founded, members began pooling their savings, extending credit to one another, and volunteering their time to operate the organization. After the separation of Elmendorf Air Force Base and Fort Richardson in 1953, Alaska USA expanded its field of membership to include military officers and enlisted personnel. The board hired its first employee in 1959. In the following ten years membership was extended to personnel assigned to remote Air Force stations in Alaska, as well as Naval Station Adak in the Aleutian Island chain.

The Member Service Center was established in 1973 to effectively serve members who

transferred out of Alaska. This was the first call center operation launched by an Alaskan financial institution, and an innovation for credit unions nationwide. Today's Member Service Center is located in Anchorage and continues to provide members throughout Alaska and around the world with toll-free telephone processing of information, service and transaction requests, seven days a week.

Alaska USA expanded beyond its military roots in 1974, when it was authorized to serve the employees of companies building the Trans-Alaska oil pipeline. In only four years, more than twenty thousand pipeline personnel opened member accounts. During this same period, the credit union's membership expanded to include ten of Alaska's Native regional corporations established under the 1971 Alaska Native Claims Settlement Act.

Alaska USA continued to expand its services and branch network, making it an attractive merger partner for smaller credit unions. Between 1979 and 1996, Alaska USA became the credit union of choice for members of six Alaska credit unions. In 1981 the Department of Defense and the National Credit Union Administration selected Alaska USA as the credit union to serve U.S. military

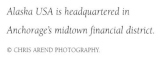

Alaska USA is headquartered in Anchorage's midtown financial district.

personnel at Clark Air Base in the Philippines. Service continued at that location until the eruption of Mount Pinatubo in 1991. Alaska USA also expanded into the Pacific Northwest in 1983 with the merger of a community-based credit union on Whidbey Island, Washington. This was followed by a merger of two Seattle-based credit unions, giving Alaska USA a strong presence in that area and enhancing geographic diversification of the credit union's membership.

Alaska USA has been responsible for introducing a number of innovations to the Alaska financial services market in order to improve and supplement its service to members. These efforts began with the formation of the Alaska Option Network in 1983, which brought shared automated teller machine (ATM) service to Alaska. Within a few years all of Alaska's major financial institutions had joined the network, which significantly expanded ATM service to Alaskans. Today there are over three hundred ATMs statewide affiliated with the Alaska Option network. Alaska USA remains the majority shareholder and operates the network.

In 1986 Alaska USA Insurance, Inc. was founded as a wholly-owned subsidiary of Alaska USA. As the number of credit and deposit products available from the credit union grew, so too did the demand for a wider variety of insurance options. This subsidiary allows the credit union to offer a broad array of insurance products and services to members on a convenient and affordable basis. Alaska USA Mortgage Company was founded in 1993 to assist Alaskans in finding the right financing to help put home ownership within reach. Alaska USA Mortgage provides comprehensive, cost-effective and professional mortgage services for the purchase or refinance of one- to four-family residential properties.

Alaska USA founded the Alaska USA Trust Company in 1997 to provide fiduciary and investment services to individuals, Alaska public units, and credit unions throughout the United States. Alaska USA Trust is the only Alaska-based provider, and the only credit union-owned and operated provider, of such services in the United States.

Since 1948, Alaska USA's commitment to its cooperative principles and the purposes for which it was chartered have remained constant. Alaska USA continues to strive to satisfy the financial needs of members from all walks of life and levels of income, providing them with the opportunity to be financially successful and to improve their standard of living.

✧

Below: Self-Service Terminals provide members with quick, easy access to their accounts.
© CHRIS AREND PHOTOGRAPHY.

Bottom: Alaska USA Federal Credit Union members can bank anywhere.

TOTEM OCEAN TRAILER EXPRESS

Totem Ocean Trailer Express (TOTE) is a privately owned Alaska Corporation operating three roll-on/roll-off (Ro/Ro) cargo steamships to Alaska between the ports of Anchorage and Tacoma, Washington. TOTE also provides for overland highway and intermodal connections throughout greater Alaska, the Lower Forty-eight and Canada. The company recently celebrated its twenty-fifth anniversary in Alaska and continues to offer superior service. As with Alaska, perseverance and resourcefulness in the face of a cyclical economy and challenging operating conditions have marked TOTE's long journey to success.

TOTE's history with Alaska began when the *Great Land*, a 790-foot long "super ship" made its inaugural voyage to Alaska from Seattle on September 10, 1975. From 1975 to 1982, TOTE was a wholly owned subsidiary of Sun Company. In 1982 TOTE's then President and CEO, Robert B. McMillen, along with a group of Pacific Northwest businessmen, formed Totem Resources Corporation (TRC) as a holding company,

and purchased TOTE from Sun. Since then, TOTE has been and continues to be a privately owned corporation. In 1987 Totem Resources Corporation purchased the Seattle-based tug and barge operation, Foss Maritime Company, from Dillingham Holdings, Inc. of San Francisco, and in 1989, Totem Resources acquired the Philadelphia-based ship management firm, Interocean Ugland Management Corporation. In 1998 Totem Resources Corporation changed its name to SaltChuk Resources. TOTE's current president, Robert P. Magee, joined the company in 1987 as vice president of Marine Operations, after four years as Senior Vice President of Vessel Operations for Puerto Rico Marine Management. Magee's association with the company dates back to its beginnings in 1975, when he was a manager at Sun Shipbuilding in Pennsylvania.

TOTE now has three Ro/Ro vessels in full-time service. These vessels accommodate wheeled cargo, which drive on and off the vessel via tractor-trailer, van or flatbed, or under its own power. One advantage of the

Ro/Ro system is the ability to speed delivery to the customer once the ship reaches port, eliminating much of the handling required for containerized or bulk cargo. Another advantage is the less restrictive freight dimensions offered by TOTE's fleet. While each of the ships has a capacity for 410 forty-foot equivalent units, the TOTE ships can accommodate virtually any size and type of cargo. Because the size and shape of freight moved aboard TOTE's ships is not limited to 20 to 45-foot containers, TOTE can offer shipping options not available from any other shipper.

In order to succeed, TOTE has had to weather some difficulties unique to the Alaskan market. When the *Great Land* sailed for Alaska in 1975, the state was enjoying prosperity brought by the height of the pipeline construction. Two years later, however, the post-pipeline economic contraction and drop in railbelt freight posed financial hardships. The market fell to its lowest point in 1979. However, a strong rebound surpassed the pipeline years as oil revenue flowed into the state's coffers. In 1986 Alaska entered a recession, which lasted nearly four years. The market rebounded, bolstered by the Exxon Valdez oil spill cleanup and more oil exploration, development of other resource industries such as seafood, coal and timber, and growth in the service sector, primarily tourism and international trade.

Also presenting major challenges to TOTE have been the physical demands of the route between Tacoma, Washington and Anchorage, Alaska. The route covers 1,450 difficult nautical miles, with seas sometimes surging to 60 feet and winds gusting at more than 75 knots during the winter. Cook Inlet can be ice-filled for more than 100 miles five months of the year. Tidal variances of up to thirty-five feet and flowing 6 to 7 knots twice a day pose a navigational challenge in crossing a shoal during each voyage. Against these odds, TOTE's three Ro/Ro vessels and crews have achieved a ninety-six percent on-time arrival record over the past five years. TOTE's line-haul trucking service also encounters challenging conditions year-round. Ice roads, avalanches and freezing temperatures attempt to impede service to the interior during the six-month winter, while thawing roadways and flash floods make for hazardous driving conditions during the balance of the year.

TOTE has announced plans to build two new Ro/Ros, which will eventually replace their three current vessels. The new ships, named the "Orca" class, will be nearly 40 feet longer and 20 feet wider than the current "Ponce" class. With these new ships, Totem Ocean Trailer Express will be well positioned for another twenty-five years of Ro/Ro service to Alaska and beyond.

PRE-CAST CONCRETE CO., INC.

❖

*Above: Pre-Cast Concrete, Inc.'s
headquarters in Anchorage.*

*Below: Pre-Cast Concrete Inc.'s
Wasilla shop.*

When founder John McGee decided to go into business for himself in 1977, he bought a book to teach him how to start a company. He knew about concrete, not business! But McGee was apparently a quick learner–his company, Pre-Cast Concrete Company, has not only survived the volatile Anchorage economy, but was awarded "The Blue Chip" by the *National Business* magazine in 1991.

McGee first came to Alaska in 1958 after completing high school. He worked odd jobs from Mount McKinley to the Kenai Peninsula. He liked Alaska, but had to return to Seattle to complete military duty and gain work experience. He was hired by Concrete Technology in Tacoma, Washington learning to make large concrete items like bridge beams, wall panels and building products–some of which were prepared for projects in Anchorage. In 1970 some products were damaged in transit to Alaska, and McGee was sent to oversee their repair.

While in Anchorage, he was asked to help Pat Stewart start Con-Stress, a large pre-stress concrete plant. "My family moved to Anchorage, bag

and baggage," says McGee. At the same time, Anchorage Sand and Gravel was starting the same type of company called Pre-Con. Both companies had to stop production by 1976. In the spring of 1977 McGee believed he could learn from the mistakes of others and started his own company, Pre-Cast Concrete Company, on April 7.

McGee's first task was to make his new company visible. He talked to contractors, the city, and telephone utilities about upcoming projects. His first big job was to build fifteen telephone vaults for Anchorage Telephone Utilities. "So we went to work," McGee remembers, "Clyde Hendrickson building the forms, Craig Losby and David Oliver building cages and pouring concrete."

By the end of 1977, Pre-Cast Concrete had established itself as a great provider of concrete products. "Anchorage was growing fast," McGee says, "but I always kept in mind the things that made the other companies fail. I tried to stay small and find work to keep us busy in the wintertime, even though we did not have a nice heated shop to work in." Borrowing money was difficult, as other companies in the same business had failed. But in 1980 McGee was able to purchase two lots on Eighty-eighth and Toloff and started making plans for a concrete shop building. McGee's plan was to build insulated concrete wall panels, a heated concrete floor and a residential apartment on top. The City of Anchorage Building Department, banks, and others were hard to sell on the idea. "With the help of Art Witmer, an engineer in Anchorage, all the hurdles were crossed. We were soon in a nice heated shop," he remembers. "I could do more and better work in the heated condition!"

Then prices fell in the mid-1980s, and Anchorage experienced a serious downturn in its economy. "I was thankful I had kept the company small," McGee remembers. "I was able to keep working when a lot of companies were going broke or downsizing." McGee saw this as a good time to expand, and it worked. Pre-Cast Concrete received an award for its approach when it was given "The Blue Chip" by National Business magazine. The article credits McGee's creative marketing, the innovative use of human resources and the company's decision to lower its profit margin to remain more competitive as reasons for its success throughout the difficult

Left: Taku Elementary School.

Below: Elmendorf Dormitory on Elmendorf Air Force Base.

economy. Not only did Pre-Cast Company survive the 1980s, it actually increased sales by expanding its product line and remaining busy during the winter.

About this time, more big changes were happening at Pre-Cast Concrete Company. The company converted to a corporation with the help of Joe Vatone and Henry Wajtusik of Tax Planners. McGee became president, son Jon, vice president; daughter Dianna, secretary; and wife Michele, treasurer.

Pre-Cast Concrete, Inc. expanded to Wasilla in 1997 by purchasing an old gravel pit and turning it into a flat area for the storage of forms. They also built a six-thousand-square-foot shop and office at 2790 Lakeview Road and started producing concrete products there.

In the year 2000 Pre-Cast Concrete, Inc. had 16 employees, 30 customers, and annual revenue of $2 million. They have a four-thousand-square-foot shop on three lots in Anchorage and a six-thousand-square-foot shop on twenty acres in Wasilla. Some of the projects completed by Pre-Cast include many recognizable sights in the city: the new Alaska Regional Native Hospital (with Ellis Don); The Century 16 Theater (with Davis Construction); the Elmendorf Air Force Base Dormitory (with Hoffman General); Tudor and Lake Otis retaining walls (with Wilder Construction); and the new Taku Elementary School (with Alcan General).

Pre-Cast Concrete, Inc. is active in the community, sponsoring events like Anchorage Recreational Basketball and the Boys and Girls Club of Anchorage.

In the future, Pre-Cast Concrete, Inc. plans to continue to provide a safe work environment for its employees and to continue to manufacture quality concrete products in shapes and sizes to fit its customers' needs.

SPINELL HOMES, INC.

❖

Above: An aerial view of a Spinell Home in a Cook Inlet neighborhood.

Below: An exterior view of a Spinell Home in a Cook Inlet neighborhood in Anchorage.

Spinell Homes started in Anchorage at one of the lowest points in the city's economic history. Through hard work and perseverance, Spinell Homes is now one of Anchorage's premiere homebuilders and one of the most recognizable names in Alaska's building industry.

Charles Spinelli founded Spinell Homes in 1987. He is a third generation builder, as his father was a bricklayer and his grandfather a stone mason on the East Coast. As Spinelli grew up, his father advised him to look for an occupation other than brick laying, as the work was hard and it was becoming a dying profession. So, Spinelli became an elementary school teacher and taught for a California school district for three years. As his family began, however, it became increasingly difficult

to make ends meet on one income, a teacher's salary. Spinelli decided to go into business with his brother-in-law, a masonry contractor in Idaho. Spinelli worked with him for two years, then went to work with Central Pre-Mix Concrete selling concrete. After two years with Central, Bowen hired him. Bowen had invented a complete foundation system, in which the floor and foundation are in one system. Spinelli spent two years selling the system, working on the product's patent, and licensing companies to manufacture the product. Spinelli first came to Alaska when Bowen sent him to Anchorage in 1984 to run its Alaska division, Bowen Quality Construction.

The company's first few years in Anchorage were moderately profitable, as about 9,000 building permits were issued in the City of Anchorage. By 1987, however, permits dropped to almost 200 as Anchorage's economic downturn all but devastated the city's building industry. Bowen Quality Construction, along with many other businesses, seemed headed for closure. Bowen asked Spinelli to leave Alaska and manage the company's Arizona division. After a trip to Arizona, Spinelli discovered that he really didn't like it as well as Alaska and decided to stick it out in Anchorage.

Spinelli started Spinell Homes in April 1987 with Bowen as a partner. However, by June 1987 it became clear that Bowen wasn't going to participate in the corporation. In 1988 Spinelli became president of Spinell Homes and took on the business of building homes in Anchorage.

It was possibly the worst time in Anchorage's history to start a home building business. People were leaving the city because of poor economic conditions and Spinelli recalls only four or five builders staying in operation during this recession. Spinelli, however, believes opening his company in those difficult times required them to develop a good focus—taking care of the customers, even in the worst of times. Spinell Homes started a regimen of construction with quality, tenets that Spinelli believes are what got Spinell Homes through the tough times and has helped make the construction company what it is today.

Spinell Homes currently has thirty-eight full-time employees, and, in 1999, the company grossed billings of over $30 million. Spinell Homes grew from sales of 24 in 1987 to sales of 167 in 1999. Spinell Homes specializes in many types of houses from those for first time homebuyers to move-up homes. They build everything from condominiums at $130,000 to more luxurious homes at around $400,000. Spinell Homes offers customers a catalog of seventy-five houses, and a wide list of options from which individual homebuyers can personalize their homes. Spinell Homes is currently working throughout Alaska and has built houses in Seward, Palmer, Wasilla, and Eagle River, as well as Anchorage. They are currently building a branch office in Palmer.

Spinell Homes is a family business. Chuck's wife, Jackie, works in the office, and son Andre is in charge of plan submissions and attaining building permits. The Spinellis also have two daughters. Lauren graduated from college in Redlands, California, in June 2001 and Lindsey graduated from West High School in Anchorage that same year. The Spinellis also think of their staff as part of the family. Spinelli credits Todd Schroder, the company's construction manager since Spinell Homes began, and Pam Woodke, office manager, as two employees who have helped make the company successful.

Because the community has supported Spinell Homes through the years, Spinelli has made a commitment to give back to the community some of that support. Spinelli is past president of the Anchorage Homebuilder Association. This year, Spinell Homes has

provided the Fourth Annual Alpine Alternatives Give-A-Way Home for raffle, which represents an in-kind donation of $50 to $80,000 to the group. Spinelli owns and maintains a field in south Anchorage for the Cook Inlet Soccer Club, of which Spinelli is a past president and current board member. Spinell Homes also makes generous donations to many other youth sports organizations.

Professional Builders' Magazine has honored Spinell Homes seven times in the last fifteen years by naming it one of the nation's top 400 revenue earning homebuilders. The *Alaska Business Monthly* has also named Spinell Homes to the "'49er" list.

✧

Above: An exterior view of a Spinell Home in Anchorage.

Below: An interior view of a Spinell Home in Anchorage.

CENTRAL PLUMBING AND HEATING

✧

Above: In 1959 no one believed Ron and Mary Cooper could start a business in a shack.

Top, right: Central Plumbing and Heating's current location at 212 East International.

Below: Plumbers protect the health of the nation.

In 1959 Alaska became a state. That same year Ron and Mary Ann Cooper started Central Plumbing and Heating (CP&H). The name was chosen because the Coopers believed that someday the location at International Airport Road and Cordova Street would be the center of town.

In May, after breakup, a former Fort Richardson hospital building was moved onto the property. It was the first business established on the road except for a service station on either end, one at Seward Highway and the other at the airport.

The company operates on simple philosophies: No job is too small and take care of the customers. Founder Ronald Cooper believes each job should be completed to the extent possible before going on to the next.

Cooper's wife, Mary Ann, attended Alaska Business College at night to learn bookkeeping, and manned the one-person front office for several years.

When plumbers and builders found they could find parts at CP&H, a retail business gradually grew. Buying at Central saved that long trip downtown.

In 1966 the current building at 212 East International was built. By then the retail business was well established. Expediting and finding supplies for customers became an appreciated service.

Mary Ann's brother, George Benson, started working summers for CP&H while attending college. After college and three years of teaching (still working at CP&H in the summer), he became a full time employee.

CP&H incorporated in 1970, with the Coopers and George and Linda Benson as shareholders.

The second generation of Coopers, sons Jeffrey and Michael, started working as teenagers in the shop and now manage the service and contracting departments. Jeffrey and Michael and their sister, Dianne Velasquez, eventually became stockholders. The company also depends heavily on its "right-hand" man, Rick Cook, who is a stockholder, and has been in charge of the retail and accounting departments since 1972.

Now, Angela Cooper, Mike's daughter, has come on board, starting the third generation of family operation.

Central Plumbing and Heating believes in supporting the community. They sponsor youth sport organizations, Habitat for Humanity, provide in-kind donations for local theater groups, and even helped build Binky's enclosure at the Anchorage Zoo.

For forty-one years the company has served the community, endeavoring to be fair to the customers and to perform the work in a professional manner.

ALASKA PUMP & SUPPLY, INC.

Alaska Pump and Supply, Inc. is a wholesale pump distributor and 'sister' corporation of Central Plumbing and Heating. George Lapp, Jim Russell, Mel Munson, and Clyde Lewis, of C. R. Lewis Company, a prominent mechanical contracting company in Anchorage, originally founded Alaska Pump in 1974. Lapp offered to sell the entire corporation's structure to George Benson, Ron Cooper, Jeff Cooper, Mike Cooper and Rick Cook in 1979. Because they were interested in attaining the inventory, the group purchased the company. They hired Barry McCormack in 1983, and later invited him to become a stockholder. Terry Gorlick and John Plovanich joined Alaska Pump into the 1990s and became stockholders in 1999.

Customer service is paramount at Alaska Pump. Finishing a job takes priority to beginning a new project, and emphasis is placed on meeting the customer's needs. The philosophy of the owners is to work with customers as though they are partners to accomplish the job at hand. This attitude has established Alaska Pump as a company that can help contractors, engineers, other distributors and equipment owners alike.

The business has grown exponentially through sales and service in the commercial, residential and industrial markets by providing good customer service. The company furnishes pumps and mechanical systems throughout the entire State of Alaska. They've sold sewer and water systems to villages, cities, school districts, and fish hatcheries. They supplied many pumps to the oil industry, including the NorthStar and Alpine projects on the North Slope. Alaska Pump is involved in the design and construction of skid-mounted pumping systems, which utilize pump-specific controls with variable frequency capabilities. These systems provide better system control and offer a substantial savings in power consumption, and thus operating costs.

Alaska Pump is also actively involved in the community, supporting youth sports programs and other charitable organizations throughout Alaska, and is pro-active in industry-affiliated organizations such as American Water Works Association, National Ground Water Association, Water Environment Federation, Alaska Miners Association, Alaska Support Industry Alliance and others.

✦

Above: Alaska Pump & Supply's corporate headquarters.

Bottom, left: This triplex constant pressure booster system was designed and built by AP&S for use in the nineteen-home Near Point Subdivision in the Stuckagain Heights area in east Anchorage. It is designed to provide 50 psi discharge with flows ranging from 1 to 225 gallons per minute.

Below: ITT Goulds model 3196X fuel transfer pumps installed at Tesoro Alaska, Port of Anchorage Tank Farm.

BLOOD BANK OF ALASKA, INC.

Medical doctors, recognizing the need for a reliable supply of blood for Alaskans, founded the Blood Bank of Alaska, Inc. (BBA) in 1962. The population of Alaska required only 682 units of blood that year. In the year 2000 Alaska's growing population has 18,000 active blood donors supplying over 20,000 units per year to 24 Alaskan hospitals!

The BBA grew gradually from one full-time employee in 1962 to thirty-one full-time employees in 1996, handling donations of 11,000 units per year. This increase could not keep up with need. In 1996 the community-based board of directors took a hard look at how to better serve the largest state in the union.

Their renewed commitment resulted in an increase of collections by twenty percent per year in the last four years. As of 2000, BBA had one hundred employees. Mobile collection teams began conducting off-site blood drives throughout the state to make donating blood more convenient. Fifty percent of collections now come from these mobile teams. This was made possible by the "LifeMobile," a forty-foot Bluebird coach purchased with donations from the Elks, Lions, and Rotary Clubs, the National Bank of Alaska, Providence Alaska Medical Center, and Alaska Regional Hospital. A Saturn wagon, also purchased by the Elks, can be pulled behind the coach. The "LifeMobile" includes quarters for staff and a musical system for use in parades.

Also new to the BBA is a state-of-the-art blood information system. Until February 2000, tens of thousands of records were handled manually. Through funds appropriated by the State of Alaska and a donation from the M. J. Murdock Charitable Trust, a new computer system was instituted which keeps all records organized and readily available to the BBA staff.

The BBA realizes that it exists solely on the goodheartedness of donors. Its exciting new reward program features an Iditarod commemorative envelope for those who donate four times a year. These "Heroes" are given an envelope like those originally carried by Joe Redington, Sr., in the 1997 Iditarod. When that supply ran out, mushers Martin Buser and Jeff King, both blood donors, volunteered to carry more of the limited edition envelopes.

Alaska's geography presents one of BBA's major challenges. In an effort to meet that challenge, BBA has established blood collection centers in Wasilla and Soldotna, as well as a blood depot in Sitka. Hospitals in the central and northern portions of the state have their blood flown in on a regular basis. The BBA's goal is to keep the blood supply adequate at all times, so Alaska is never faced with a shortage.

The Anchorage Museum Association (AMA), which was originally called the Anchorage Fine Arts Museum Association, had its beginnings in 1969; one year after the Museum opened its doors. Its founders, many of whom are still involved with the Museum today, felt strongly that private support of the Museum was as essential as Municipal support in order to build a flourishing Museum. Because of their efforts, the Museum began as the private/public partnership which continues to this day with the AMA as the 501(c)(3) private, not-for-profit arm of the Anchorage Museum of History and Art.

Our supporters are passionate and devoted to preserving Alaska's art and culture as reflected by the more than $1.5 million raised each year for the Museum. One of the AMA's outstanding accomplishments is the Anchorage Museum Shop, which donates a generous part of its profit from sales of the highest quality art and crafts, books about Alaska art and history and items related to the Museum's collections. Another source of funding is through the sale of memberships, which now number 4,589. Members of the Museum receive free admission to the Museum, a bimonthly newsletter, discounts in the Museum Shop and Café and invitations to special events.

The AMA also organizes two major fundraising events every year—Beaujolais Nouveau held each November and a gala dinner and art auction held in the spring. Private and corporate gifts have been vital to the success of the Museum as one of Alaska's premier cultural landmarks. The AMA also raises funds through foundation, corporate and individual gifts, which account for $450,000 in the annual budget.

A dedicated staff of ten people works closely with the Museum staff of thirty to accomplish the goals of both the AMA and the Museum. The AMA staff is largely concerned with preserving the integrity and life of the museum through development activities, community involvement and education, which complements the work of the curatorial staff. AMA funds are essential to support acquisitions for the collections, conservation, educational programming and exhibitions, while Municipal funds are used for staffing and maintaining the Museum facility.

The AMA is particularly proud of its accomplishments in funding the development of many of the Museum's temporary exhibitions. The AMA supports an ongoing series of solo and group exhibitions by Alaska artists, an annual interactive exhibition for children and families, an annual statewide juried art exhibition, and a major summer exhibition with an Alaska theme. Among the most important have been "Our Way of Making Prayers: The Living Tradition of Yup'ik Masks" and "Science Under Sail: Russia's Great Voyages to America 1728-1867."

The most recent project of the AMA is this book, *Historic Anchorage: An Illustrated History*. We hope you will enjoy learning about Anchorage as you read through this book. If you are interested in learning more about the Anchorage Museum of History and Art and the Anchorage Museum Association, please visit our website, www.anchoragemuseum.org, or write to us at 121 West Seventh Avenue; Anchorage, AK 99501. We welcome your interest and comments.

ANCHORAGE MUSEUM ASSOCIATION

✧

Above: Museum Art Instructor Steve Gordon shares his knowledge with schoolchildren.

Below: The heritage of other cultures is often featured in the museum's temporary exhibits and programs.

CARLILE TRANSPORTATION SYSTEMS

Carlile Transportation Systems is a real Alaskan success story. John and Harry McDonald, brothers from Seward, Alaska, founded it in 1980. They had two tractors and years of experience hauling timber, milk, bulk products and general freight throughout Alaska. Their expertise and understanding of the unique demands of Alaska's terrain and special needs of its residents helped transform their operation into a full service transportation and logistics company which serves customers throughout Alaska, Canada and the Lower Forty-eight.

Owner Jeff Allen became involved with the company with the addition of the LTL division in 1983. Linda Leary and Karl Hoenack became owners in 1994 shortly after the addition of the K&W Transportation division. In early 1999, Carlile moved into a newly built terminal in Anchorage, consolidating its four buildings and the small shop, which it had previously occupied. The impressive growth experienced by Carlile has been made possible by a combination of strong managerial leadership, modern equipment, and an emphasis on providing the best possible service to the customer at the lowest possible cost.

In 1997 Carlile purchased the old Mark Air facility in Deadhorse, Alaska. This facility allows Carlile to be the only full-service carrier in Prudhoe Bay, with truck and air handling capabilities. Along with the Prudhoe Bay

facility, Carlile also has terminals in Anchorage, Fairbanks, Kenai, Seward, Federal Way, Washington and Edmonton, Alberta, Canada.

Carlile Transportation Systems is an Alaskan-owned company offering cost-effective pricing options, multi-modal service, on-site technical assistance, customized reports, and a twenty-four-hour emergency crew. Carlile offers four weekly departures from Washington and Alaska, and freight can be moved from most points within the Continental United States in less than a week. It also offers daily service to Anchorage, Seward, Kenai, Homer, Prudhoe Bay and Fairbanks in Alaska. The company's outstanding service is made possible by its commitment to provide the best equipment available today, including flatbeds, reefer vans, tankers and other specialized equipment. Its newest acquisition, the Cozad Lowboy, offers a capacity of 125 tons, more than double that of previous lowboys. Carlile also employs state-of-the-art technological advances, which improve efficiency and safety, such as on-board computers and electronically controlled engines in tractors making the trip from Fairbanks to Prudhoe Bay, saving 60 to 80 gallons of fuel per trip.

Carlile employs 375 people in Alaska and 40 in Seattle. Carlile supports the community through the United Way, Alaska Food Bank, and the Alaska Trucking Association, among others.

❖
Below: Carlile Transportation Systems Headquarters in Anchorage, Alaska.

HUNTER FISHER
TAXIDERMY, INC.

When Hunter Fisher stuffed his first Brooks Rainbow trout for customer Ken Guffey in 1964, he launched one of Anchorage's first and most reliable taxidermy businesses. After all, with a name like Hunter Fisher, is it any wonder he ended up in the taxidermy business?

Fisher was born in West Virginia. His job as a federal investigator for the civil service, which he held for twenty-five years, brought him to Anchorage in 1962. During his investigative career, fishing and taxidermy were his hobbies. After retiring, he opened a taxidermy shop in Old Spenard at 1111 Chugach Drive. He later moved the shop to a location near Arctic and International, near the current shop's location at 822 West International Airport Road. Fisher touched the lives of many Alaskans by listening to their tall fishing tales, promoting the Alaska Sport Fisherman's Association, and providing quality taxidermy. Many customers still enjoy his work today, including a mounted fish that is now twenty-five years-old. Alaskans lost a great friend when Fisher died on July 16, 1998.

Fisher had sold the business to Tom Elias in 1987. Elias owned the store for twelve years, during which time he added mammals to Hunter Fisher Taxidermy services. Current owner Tom Buckmeier bought Hunter Fisher Taxidermy, Inc. on June 2,1999. Buckmeier is a life-long Alaskan, born in the old Providence Hospital on "L" Street in Anchorage. His father moved to Alaska in 1962 and taught in the Anchorage School District for twenty-two years. Buckmeier joined his father on many hunting trips. "I grew up in the back of my Dad's Super Cab," he laughs. He also learned to appreciate taxidermy by spending a great deal of time as a kid in the shop of friend Lonnie Temple, a well-known Anchorage taxidermist. As an adult, Buckmeier enjoys hunting as a hobby, particularly sheep hunting. When he heard Hunter Fisher Taxidermy was up for sale, it seemed a natural step for him to change his career as an X-ray technician with Dr. David Kyzer and purchase the shop.

Buckmeier looks forward to continuing Hunter Fisher's tradition of quality taxidermy and customer service. He has also continued Hunter Fisher's commitment to the community by supporting Safari Club International, Ducks Unlimited, Alaska Peace Officers Corps, Alaska Chapter of North American Wild Sheep, Rocky Mountain Elks Foundation, National Senior Services Corps of Alaska (Foster Grandparents), and the Jewel Lake Ice Fishing Jamboree for the Disabled.

❖

Above: Hunter Fisher in his first shop at this home in Spenard.

Below: Tom Buckmeier after a successful hunt on Kodiak Island.

FALTZ LANDSCAPING, INC.

✧

*Above: James and Teresa Faltz with sons,
eight-year-old Storm and five-year-old
Hunter, November 2000.*

*Below: Residential landscaping near
Campbell Lake, Anchorage, Alaska.*

creative and unique designs to improve the quality and esthetics of the exterior construction in Anchorage.

James A. Faltz, who moved to Anchorage in 1984 from Sarasota, Florida, founded the company in 1992. In 1984, after moving to Anchorage, he married his childhood sweetheart, Teresa, who had moved from Florida to Alaska in 1976. The couple has two children, Hunter, age five, and Storm, age eight.

Faltz, a third generation landscaper, learned his craft helping his father, James B. Faltz, a landscaper and excavator in Florida. His first job in Anchorage was with Bush Landscaping, a well-respected landscape and nursery company. He worked with Jeff Dillon, a landscape architect, for seven years before starting his own company. James' mother, Mary K. Faltz, who worked as a bookkeeper for UIC, a construction company in Barrow, and other companies, gave Faltz Landscaping, the financial knowledge needed to start a new business. Mary passed away in 1998 from cancer and is sorely missed.

Faltz Landscaping, Inc. and Faltz Deck and Patio Builders (FLI) specialize in computer landscape design and installation, deck and patio design and installation and landscaping services including annual flower design and installation, lawn irrigation, landscape lighting, decorative retainer walls, lawn maintenance, and consultation. In 2000 FLI entered the retail nursery business by offering large ornamental trees and shrubs hardy to Alaska. Its mission is to provide landscaping and deck and patio construction in a professional manner utilizing

FLI is located at 7010 Old Seward Highway. It started with five seasonal employees and approximately 20 residential clients to 40 seasonal and year-round employees with over 120 residential and commercial clients. Residential projects consist of simple lawn spring clean-ups to complete new landscapes. Commercial projects can consist of small buildings to large department stores. FLI has grown an average of twenty percent a year, and is now one of the largest landscape companies in Anchorage. FLI provides services for some of Anchorage's prominent long-time residents, including Larry Carr and Barney Gottstein of Carr-Gottstein Properties and Gary Baugh of Baugh Construction.

FLI implements a personal business theory of "quality before profits" and has realized a strong demand for its services due to repeat clients and client referrals. They have received numerous awards, including the 1998 Celebration of Anchorage Awards; first place City of Flowers Mayor's award; first place fifteen-year maintenance award for work at the Calais Office Center; and first place TREEmendous Anchorage Mayor's award for the BP Exploration Building.

Faltz Landscaping looks forward to doing business in Anchorage for many years to come.

Alaska Wild Berry Products (AWBP) has been called the Disneyland of the north based upon the magic visitors experience when they walk through the doors of the Main Store at 5225 Juneau Street, Anchorage, Alaska. The company has grown dramatically from its humble beginnings in Homer, Alaska. In 1946 Kenneth and Hazel Heath began making jams and jellies in their kitchen with the wild berries of Alaska picked near their home. Today, just as in 1946, berry pickers in the wilderness of Alaska compete with bears to harvest the wild berries used by AWBP to produce its exclusive line of jams, jellies, syrups, sauces, and chocolates.

The mission of the owner, Peter Eden, is to give customers a memorable and enchanting experience. Eden purchased the company in 1975. In 1987 he launched the company into a major phase of development. This expansion included an upgrade in factory equipment to increase production in jams and jellies, and expand the candy line. It was at this time that Eden introduced chocolate-covered wild berry jelly center chocolates, and a wide variety of other chocolate-covered candies.

Eden continually upgrades the company's retail facilities. AWBP has three retail stores, one in Homer and two in Anchorage. In addition,

AWBP has a thriving mail order business through its annual catalog, and the company's web page found at www.alaskawildberryproduct.com.

The Main Store is famous around the world for its chocolate "waterfall." The falls contain thirty-four hundred pounds of melted chocolate that cascade from twenty feet in the air through sparkling copper kettles. Hence, the reason Eden is affectionately known as Willy Wonka.

AWBP and Eden have been the recipients of many awards recognizing the outstanding nature of the business and its products. In 1989 Eden received the Alaska Small Businessperson of the Year Award from the U.S. Small Business Administration. The Anchorage Economic Development Corporation presented the Hometown Investor Award to AWBP in 1994.

Retail Confectioners International (RCI) gave the awards for which Eden beams with pride. In 1999 AWBP won RCI's Gold Bowl for Best of Show. In 1998 and 1999 awards were received for chocolate pieces created by Victoria Wright, age nine, the world's youngest chocolate connoisseur. In 1998 AWBP and Victoria received RCI's highly esteemed Silver Bowl for Victoria's Caramels in the category Best New Piece. Victoria's next creation was Moose Nuggets. This piece won the Silver Bowl in the category Best Summer Candy in 1999. Eden believes that when it comes to candy, listen to a child, and Victoria is an expert.

ALASKA WILD BERRY PRODUCTS, INC.

✧

Above: The famous chocolate waterfall at Alaska Wild Berry in Anchorage, Alaska.

Below: Alaska Wild Berry store located at 5225 Juneau in Anchorage, Alaska.

SHIMEK & COMPANY, INC.

When Robert Shimek came to Anchorage, Alaska during World War II, he had no plans to stay in that isolated, rustic little town, but he came to believe that Alaska would offer great economic opportunity after the war. The business he started in 1945 has gone through many changes in product lines, technology, name and locations, but exists to this day as Shimek's Audio and Video and Metro Music and Book.

Robert was born in White Bear Lake, Minnesota in 1914. He came to Anchorage to do war-related technical work for the Federal Aviation Administration and Northwest Airlines. During the war he corresponded with a young woman named Violet working in a defense plant back in Minnesota, and when the war ended she came north to marry Robert and assist him in starting a retail business–selling and repairing small appliances and radios. Over the following ten years the couple had four children—Joseph, David, Roberta, and Terry—while nurturing their growing business. By the early 1950s Robert and Vi were selling stereo

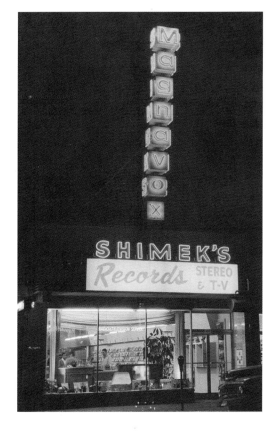

phonographs and recordings; television came to Anchorage in 1953 and Shimek's Radio expanded and flourished. Vi and Robert worked side by side in the business through the years; Robert managed the "hard goods" while Vi had charge of recorded music—45s, LP records, eight-tracks, and cassettes.

The business changed locations many times, usually to allow for growth. But in 1964 the business was forced to move because it was destroyed in the disastrous earthquake that struck Anchorage that spring. A few years later, Robert passed active management of the businesses to his oldest son Joe, and thereafter Robert and Vi devoted more and more of their time to travel and golf. Sons David and Terry took on the businesses in the 90s. (Daughter Roberta and her husband Craig Ketchum own and operate another Anchorage business institution—Ketchum Air Service).

Robert Shimek died in 1995 at the age of eighty. Violet continues to "report for duty" to the family business each day and remains an integral part of operations, helping the Shimek sons carry on their father's legacy. They hope to hand over that legacy to the next generation in a few years.

✧

Right: Shimek's Records, Stereo & TV, downtown Anchorage, 1954-1964. The store was totally demolished in the 1964 Good Friday Earthquake.

Below: Robert Shimek, c. early 1950s.

RAIN PROOF ROOFING COMPANY, INC.

The success of a company in Alaska depends a great deal upon the variety of jobs it is willing to perform. At Rain Proof Roofing Company, Inc. the sky is the limit, whether your project is a home or a large commercial building.

Jack and Vi Markley, serving Anchorage's residential building industry, founded the company in 1962. As Anchorage grew and expanded so did Rain Proof, which now serves residential, commercial, industrial and public builders. Rain Proof installs several types of roofing and waterproofing systems, including metal, single-ply, built-up, and shingles.

Rain Proof is currently owned and operated by the Markley's daughter and son-in-law, April and Pat Reilly. The Reillys started working at Rain Proof in 1973 full-time, became its managers in 1978 and purchased the business in 1983. Rain Proof was first located on Barrow Street off of Fireweed Lane. As the company grew it relocated to 2201 East 84th Court. The Reillys believe strongly in customer service and the diversity that Rain Proof offers. These are the company's strongest selling points. While the company works on many small projects, it also accommodates large jobs, including the Military Mall on Elmendorf Air Force Base. Its seven-acre roof is Anchorage's largest.

No place in the state is too remote for Rain Proof. They have worked on projects in Interior Alaska, the Arctic Region, Kenai Peninsula, Southeast, and the Aleutian Chain. Projects include Spring Creek Correctional Facility in Seward; Elmendorf Air Force Base Hospital, Medical Examiner's Facility; Costco, K-Mart, and Wal-Mart stores; and numerous Anchorage and Fairbanks schools.

In 1993 Rain Proof received a prestigious award from Carlisle SynTec Systems of Carlisle, Pennsylvania, a manufacturer of single-ply roof systems. Company representatives distributed the award through a rigorous quality control process including on-site inspections. Carlisle awarded Rain Proof the Centurion Award as a result of 100 projects being graded a perfect ten, which was the first award of its kind given to a roofing company west of the Rockies. Again in 1998 Rain Proof became a member of Carlisle's "250" Hall of Fame, after 250 consecutive projects were graded a perfect ten.

Rain Proof advocates supporting the local community by purchasing supplies and equipment locally. Rain Proof also strongly supports community organizations such as the Boys and Girls Clubs of Anchorage, Habitat for Humanity, YMCA, Bean's Café and the United Way.

Providing good customer service and high quality of workmanship are two attributes highly valued by Rain Proof's employees and management personnel.

❖

Above: Rain Proof Roofing yard and operations center.

Below: Rain Proof Roofing, Company, Inc. is located at 2201 East 84th Court in Anchorage, Alaska.

UNIVERSITY OF ALASKA ANCHORAGE

✧

Below: The Business Education Building in the summertime.

Bottom: UAA's modern student housing is home to nearly one thousand students.

While the U.S. Congress established the University of Alaska as a land grant college in 1915, the evolution of state supported higher education in Anchorage and south-central Alaska did not begin until 1953 when Anchorage Community College first opened its doors to first- and second-year students.

As the state grew, so did the needs in Anchorage. In the late 1960s, upper level courses were offered through Anchorage Senior College, and in the mid-1970s, the four-year University of Alaska Anchorage (UAA) received full accreditation from the Northwest Council of Schools and Colleges.

A major restructuring of the University of Alaska Statewide System of Higher Education occurred in 1987. UAA and ACC merged and were joined by Kenai Peninsula College, Kodiak College, Matanuska-Susitna College and Prince William Sound Community College to create one of three major academic units (MAUs) in Alaska. Campus construction in Anchorage began in 1966 with a statewide university bond issue funding the first five buildings, named in honor of Eugene Short, Beatrice McDonald, Lucy Cuddy, Gordon Hartlieb, and Sally Monserud.

Construction of the College of Arts and Sciences and Library buildings began in the early 1970s. The Library developed as a consortium between ACC, UAA, and Alaska Methodist University. Later in the 1970s, the Performing Arts Center (renamed the Wendy Williamson Auditorium) opened, as did the campus center/sports facility/bookstore complex, and others. The Merrill Field Aviation Complex and the UAA Fine Arts and Administration Buildings were built in the 1980s. The 1990s brought on-line the three-story Business Education Building and UAA's $33-million campus housing project consisting of three, four-story residence halls and a dining/support facility.

Five teaching units form the core of UAA's academic mission: the College of Business and Public Policy; the College of Arts and Sciences; the Community and Technical College; the College of Health, Education, and Social Welfare (which includes the School of Education and School of Nursing), and the School of Engineering. UAA is now the largest, most comprehensive university in the state, offering instruction at its four primary campuses and at numerous other sites throughout South-central Alaska, the Aleutian Chain and at military facilities statewide. UAA offers associate, baccalaureate, and masters degrees, as well as vocational and professional certificates in more than 115 major study areas. The University also provides adult basic education and GED classes. The UAA Seawolf student athletes are top performers in and out of the classroom. The Department of Theatre and Dance is among the nation's best. UAA is a significant cultural resource for the Anchorage area.

NINE STAR ENTERPRISES, INC.

Where is the ninth star? Beyond the eight stars on Alaska's flag, every customer who enters one of Nine Star's training centers becomes at that moment the most important star in the company's constellation. Like the individual stars that make significant changes in their lives as they complete a training program, Nine Star grew in different ways from its inception in 1975 through the turn of the millennium. Today it represents the interests and goals of three thousand-plus youths and adults annually as they move toward skills levels that make them marketable in the new economy.

At one end of the company's galaxy, Nine Star offers basic skills education and employment training to men and women seeking to achieve their highest potential. Located in the Mountain View, Muldoon, Fairview, and Downtown neighborhoods, Nine Star centers are convenient for many of the Anchorage residents using these instructional services. Cooperating with area wide businesses, Nine Star creates great employment opportunities for people entering the workforce.

For those already in stable employment, training in technology offers opportunities for job advancement and increased productivity. Computer skills lead to certifications and provide high quality instruction from beginning to advanced applications. Nine Star delivers training at one of its modern laboratories or where the learner works.

Nine Star's organizational development services cover topics from technical communications to corporate stewardship. Strategic planning, team development, and meeting facilitation lead to better performance, and Nine Star's trainers use effective, learner oriented instructional strategies to make these topics relevant to business people who want to boost productivity. Senior trainers David S. Alexander, Carol L. Northamer, and Susan

Taylor Alling work with companies and agencies throughout Alaska.

Dr. Alexander, the company's president, and Dr. Milburn Nelson, Nine Star Development Director, design modern training programs that make effective use of current technology. Nine Star is synonymous with excellence in training, and its high school equivalency program under Vice President Northamer's direction represents the best of the company's twenty-five-year tradition of customer service.

Nine Star's leadership team includes long time Alaskans Linda Hulbert, Mary Wondzell, Jerry Smetzer, and Leonard Hamilton. The company also sponsors, supervises and trains AmeriCorps and VISTA members. Partnering through the Anchorage Job Centers, Nine Star provides basic skills, work search, and case management services to youth and adults. The Muldoon Job Center houses the English Literacy Institute, and youth programs take place at the Mountain View Job Center. The well being of thousands of satisfied people who have used Nine Star's services reflects the company's success.

✧

Above: Individual attention for individual learners.

Below: Nine Star's leaders are long-time Alaskan residents.

GCI

The story of GCI, the company that brought long-distance competition to Alaska, serves as a model of what is happening in telecommunications today. Alaska is a unique and challenging market in which to provide telecommunications services. It is remote and vast, yet small in population. Anchorage has the largest population in Alaska and passes more telecommunication traffic than anywhere else in the state.

GCI was founded in 1979 by Alaskan entrepreneurs Robert Walp and Ronald Duncan, the first and current presidents of GCI, respectively. It all began in a small Anchorage apartment in Bootleggers' Cove, when Duncan and Walp discussed the challenges of bringing affordable, state-of-the-art telecommunications technology to Alaska. Their dream became a reality on Thanksgiving Day in 1982, when GCI entered into the long distance market. Telephone rates fell drastically almost overnight. GCI has grown into what it is known for today—a premiere integrated telecommunications company providing local, wireless, long-distance, telephone, cable television, Internet, and data communication services.

GCI's heritage to Anchorage and the State of Alaska has been to bring competition to the telecommunications field. GCI's role in the Alaskan communication revolution has been a significant one, investing $750 million in integrated communication assets within the last ten years. Positioning itself to become the premiere ICP in Alaska, GCI has combined all the assets necessary to deliver voice, video, and data communication services.

The success of GCI reflects the strong leadership of the two men whose idea started it all. Walp, although officially retired from GCI in 1989, joined the board of directors and still plays an active role in company affairs. He helped guide the development of commercial satellite communication services throughout Alaska, first as a consultant to the governor's office of telecommunications and later as director of that office by appointment from Governor Jay Hammond in 1975.

Duncan has been president and CEO since 1989. Prior to starting GCI, Duncan founded and was president of Alaskavision, an Alaska-based cable television company.

GCI has a vibrant future in Alaska. It has potential to benefit more than most states from the communication revolution because of new technologies and changing regulatory policies in Alaska. Competitive advantage in the future will occur in places with raw materials for cyber-commerce and a high quality of life. Alaskans have both of these advantages, and they will aid GCI's delivery of its vision—to create value for its customers, opportunities for its employees and growth for its shareholders.

✧

Robert Walp, one of the founders and the first president of GCI, standing near GCI's satellite dish at its Anchorage headquarters location.

HIEBERT ENTERPRISES, INC.

Alaska is a land known for pioneers and pioneer spirit. Without such brave individuals, Alaska would still be a remote destination, cut off by distance from the rest of the world. But Alaska is in touch—and we have pioneers like August G. "Augie" Hiebert to thank for that!

Augie is a humble, soft-spoken man who doesn't see himself as a hero. He will tell you that he was just fortunate enough to bring the right skills to the right place at the right time in technological history. Hiebert moved to Alaska from Oregon to work at KFAR in Fairbanks in 1939 as an engineer. For the next three-and-a-half years, Augie and Stan Bennett, his boss, worked and lived inside the station and its one-bedroom apartment. Augie, also a ham radio operator, was the first Alaskan to hear about the attack on Pearl Harbor. On December 7, 1941, he was recording short wave transmissions at KFAR when he heard the news. After confirming the devastating information, he alerted the commander of Ladd Air Force Base, who notified the Alaska Defense Command.

KFAR's owner, the legendary Alaskan "Cap" Lathrop, transferred Augie to Anchorage in 1947 to build his radio station KENI. After Lathrop's death in 1950, Hiebert decided to put his energy into bringing television to Alaska. Augie filed for the first FCC television license in Alaska in May 1953 and received construction permits for the television station in July 1953. KTVA was located in the fourteen-story Mount McKinley Building. On December 11, 1953, KTVA began broadcasting as Alaska's first television station. Augie was determined to bring television to Fairbanks–he was successful when KTVF began broadcasting in February 1955.

Through the years, Augie met dignitaries such as Werner von Braun and Walter Cronkite, who wrote the introduction to *Airwaves Over Alaska*, a biography of Augie written by his daughter, Robin Ann Chlupach. He has also received many awards recognizing him for both technological innovations and community service. His most recent innovation, however, is one of which he is most proud. In December 2000, he received Alaska's highest honor, the "Alaska Legion of

✧

August G. "Augie" Hiebert.

Merit" for developing an emergency information system to 241 Alaskan villages that did not receive radio or TV signals. This innovation has the potential for saving thousands of lives.

Augie "retired" in March 1997 when he sold Northern Television, Inc. He developed Hiebert Enterprises as a way to distribute his legacy to his four daughters, three nieces, and a nephew.

ALASKA TRUST COMPANY

President and CEO Douglas Blattmachr of Alaska Trust Company.

PHOTO COURTESY OF CLARK JAMES MISHLER.

Alaska has always been a place for developing new ways of thinking and doing things. When friends approached Douglas Blattmachr about starting a trust company in Alaska, the state's current trust laws were not a deterrent. They went to work to change them, and today, Blattmachr is president of Alaska Trust Company, the first independent trust company in Alaska.

The whole idea for Alaska Trust Company began on an Alaskan fishing trip. Doug and his wife were discussing with friends how much they wanted to move back to Alaska. Doug had almost thirty years of trust experience in all aspects of trust administration and investments, including chief investment officer for a $5 billion trust company in Idaho. The goal was to create a financial services industry built around trust and investment services.

To make Alaska Trust Company a reality, the Blattmachrs would move back to Alaska. Doug would utilize his talents and work to revise trust laws to help Alaska's economy to diversify from oil and mining into an industry that wouldn't have any negative impacts on the environment. Jonathan Blattmachr, Esquire, Doug's brother, first had the idea of working with the state legislature to change those laws. Although Alaska had statutes for the formation of a trust company on its books for forty years, no independent trust company was in existence. In addition, the group needed to draft legislation and present it to the legislature. Jonathan drafted the Alaska Trust Act and, with the help of local trust & estate attorneys, CLUs, etc., was able to get the Act passed, establish a trust company, and eventually make additional changes to Alaska's trust laws. It took over four years to accomplish these tasks.

Alaska Trust Company opened its doors to customers in April 1997. It is the only native held trust company in America, as it is seventy-three percent owned by The Aleut Corporation. Alaska Trust Company now offers sixteen unique trust products and customized investment management services to customers. Alaska Trust Company credits its excellent staff with the firm's growth and success. With hard work and the foresight of both the Legislature and the governor's office, Alaska Trust Company was able to accomplish their goals, and to make Alaska the premiere jurisdiction for trust services. Alaska Trust Company is more competitive than similar companies in other states because it is independent and can be more responsive than trust companies affiliated with larger institutions. Alaska Trust Company also delivers information to clients in new convenient venues, including its website www.alaskatrust.com, informative CDs, and video.

Life in Alaska's remote villages was very different thirty years ago. There was typically no electricity, no central water supply, no adequate housing or other amenities enjoyed by residents of urban areas. A few Native leaders recognized the key to progress in their communities was the establishment of electrical systems. In 1967 the Alaska Village Electric Cooperative, Inc. (AVEC) was formed and, today, provides electricity for fifty-one remote Alaskan villages. The non-profit cooperative's mission is to provide quality electric utility service to rural Alaska villages and assist its members in improving the quality of life in their communities.

AVEC began operations in 1968 with three villages and has continued to grow over the past thirty-two years in spite of some difficult times in the 1970s. Inflation, major oil price increases, as well as new environmental laws and regulations made AVEC's first decade a real struggle. Further aggravating the situation in Alaska was the rapid construction of the Trans-Alaska Pipeline with huge injections of capital spending in a state with no private industry history of handling a project of this magnitude. Also, many AVEC employees left to take much higher paying jobs on the Pipeline, creating gaps in the fledgling organization.

Through creativity, trial and error, and old-fashioned perseverance, the founding board members of AVEC pursued their goal. Their fledgling organization has become a

successful business model for organizations endeavoring to provide a complete service to their communities. Currently, twenty-two thousand Alaskans rely on electricity provided by AVEC. Their villages were previously supported by the State of Alaska at their expense. AVEC succeeded in helping them break that cycle of dependency. One way in which AVEC is able to offer reliable service is through developing a skilled cadre of workers in the villages. Villages retain ownership through hiring and supervision of over one hundred local plant operators.

Today's AVEC headquarters is at 4831 Eagle Street in Anchorage. Sixty persons work full-time in the headquarters. AVEC hosts a major annual meeting of delegates bringing over one hundred village members to Anchorage for the two-day session in March. AVEC purchases over $14 million annually in fuel, supplies, and services, primarily in Anchorage. AVEC's Anchorage-based employees represent over $4 million in payroll injected into the local economy.

AVEC actively supports local community events, and provides over $20,000 in annual scholarships for village students. AVEC works actively with State Legislature and other agencies to promote rural funding and economic development. AVEC has been named a partner of the federal/state Denali Commission, building infrastructure in rural Alaska.

ALASKA VILLAGE ELECTRIC COOPERATIVE, INC.

✧

Above: Children playing in one of the fifty-one Alaskan villages AVEC serves.

Below: An example of subsistence lifestyle in an Alaskan village.

DOWLAND-BACH CORP.

Lynn Johnson, president of Dowland-Bach Corporation, remembers the exact moment the company was founded—7:45 a.m., May 19, 1975. Longtime friend Ed Clinton, inventor and entrepreneur, gathered Johnson and Ron Tharp at his kitchen table to discuss creation of a company that could provide fail-safe wellhead and flowline protection products to the North Slope. The group started Dowland-Bach Corporation, which has provided quality stainless steel products and safety control systems to Alaskans ever since.

Clinton's original idea was to manufacture safety systems and panels here in Alaska for the Prudhoe Bay oil fields on the North Slope because, in the 1970s, no one was manufacturing systems and panels for use in the sub-zero Arctic climate. Clinton's proposal was to build them here in Alaska, where they were to be used. The concept caught on quickly. BP originally contracted them to create seventy-two wellhead safety systems. Currently, several thousand Dowland-Bach "Wellhead Control Systems" have been installed and are in use in extreme locations from the North Slope to South America.

Alaska's petroleum industry has changed in the twenty-five years since the organization of Dowland-Bach, in turn changing and expanding the scope of their products and services. The petroleum industry has attempted

Above: BP Milne Point Wellhead Safety System.

Below: BP Colombia Solar-Powered Wellhead System.

to reduce the size of its production facilities in order to reduce costs without compromising production. Dowland-Bach has met those needs by fabricating custom hydraulic-pneumatic equipment support structures and enclosures of various sizes and configurations. Specialty fabrication of stainless panels, chemical injection systems, electrical enclosures as well as specialty stainless steel items have been added over the years to supplement the oil field focus. The fishing industry, residential and commercial custom stainless items have also become product lines. Their major clients include BP Exploration Alaska, Phillips Alaska Inc., Alyeska Pipeline, BP-Colombia, Veco, and Cominco. Dowland-Bach is also an Underwriter's Laboratories-listed panel shop with capabilities of producing UL508 Industrial Control Panels and UL-698 Industrial Control Panels for hazardous environments.

The company can manufacture practically any stainless steel item in its twenty-thousand-square-foot Anchorage warehouse. This list includes—but is not limited to—the design and manufacturing of solar-powered industrial control systems, custom kitchen equipment, handrails, column cladding, sinks, countertops and store fronts. The company's "unofficial" slogan is "Stainless 'R Us," and its employees carry stainless steel business cards to prove it.

Dowland-Bach sticks to its original concept, "Buy Alaskan, Employ Alaskan and Build Alaska" and makes the customer its top priority.

Wohlforth, Vassar, Johnson & Brecht was established in Anchorage in 1968 and became a prominent firm with a statewide practice and national recognition as a public finance firm. The firm started with Eric Wohlforth working on bond issues of the greater Anchorage area borough and the Alaska State Housing Authority in the late 1960s. Since then the firm has served as bond counsel for all state agencies and most Alaska municipal issuers of bonds for over thirty-two years.

Indeed, during the 1990s the firm placed sixth nationally among bond counsel in giving opinions on housing issues and first in one of those years in approving taxable municipal issues.

The firm does far more than public finance and has a wide experience as counsel to public entities such as the City of Seward, the University of Alaska, and the Alaska State Public Investment Board and has built a broad and comprehensive business, commercial, including securities and government law practice.

The eight attorneys of Wohlforth, Vassar, Johnson & Brecht are evenly balanced between public finance law on the one hand and municipal/commercial law on the other. The senior partners have closely identified with the State of Alaska and municipal government since the firm's inception. Eric Wohlforth was commissioner of revenue between 1970 and 1972 and has served on the Alaska Permanent Fund Corporation Board of Trustees since 1995 during which he served as chairman for two years as well. Robert Johnson, who has been with the firm

nineteen years, was an assistant attorney general and director of petroleum revenue for the Alaska Department of Revenue. Kenneth Vassar, an eighteen-year attorney, has served as assistant attorney general and with the Legislative Affairs Agency as legislative draftsman. Julius Brecht, shareholder since 1986, served as director of the Division of Banking, Securities, and Corporations. He concentrates in securities and corporate law. Cynthia Cartledge serves as primary bond counsel for the Municipality of Anchorage and the Alaska Municipal Bond Bank.

The firm is unique in providing the kind of public finance service typically available only in large cities directly in Alaska and for Anchorage clients, and in providing a municipal and commercial practice tailored to Alaska.

WOHLFORTH, VASSAR, JOHNSON & BRECHT

❖

The partners of Wohlforth, Vassar, Johnson & Brecht.

EVERGREEN MEMORIAL CHAPELS

Evergreen Memorial Chapel began its tradition of Alaskans helping Alaskans in 1957. Dedication to families in grief has helped establish Evergreen as the largest and most trusted funeral home in Alaska.

R. J. "Dave" Franke and wife, Eleanor, founded Evergreen in 1957. Dave had lived in Anchorage since 1952, and Eleanor since 1953. The original facility was located at the corner of Fourth Avenue and Barrow Street in downtown Anchorage. This facility left much to be desired as it was originally an old bar that had been converted into a funeral home. In 1958 the Frankes' decided to build the first "ground-up" funeral home in Alaska and purchased property at the corner of Eighth Avenue and "E" Street where the main chapel is located today.

Richard "Dick" Rome joined the Frankes' as their first full-time licensed employee in 1959. In 1962 the Frankes built another funeral home at the corner of Wyoming Drive and Spenard Road, called Spenard Heights Mortuary. This facility was later known as Evergreen Funeral Home and Crematory and now as the Alaska Cremation Center. In 1965 the crematory unit was purchased, again a first for Alaska. Dick was made partner in the family-owned business in 1970. In June 1985 Scott Janssen joined the staff as the first new hire in many years. In May 1988 Dave suffered a heart attack. Anchorage lost an excellent funeral director and a great friend.

Eleanor Franke and Dick Rome continued to operate the funeral home, making some internal changes in the building and adding additional garage and office space. Scott introduced an advanced planning program in 1989 to allow families to pre-fund and/or preplan their funeral arrangements.

In the spring of 1992, Evergreen joined The Loewen Group International, a group of over 400 independent funeral homes. Dick managed Evergreen until retiring on June 1, 1994, whereupon Scott Janssen became general manager. Janssen, a graduate of the Mortuary Science Department from the University of Minnesota, undertook remodeling Evergreen's facilities to make them more comfortable for grieving families and loved ones. In 1996 the Spenard location was remodeled to better serve families choosing cremation. In July 1997 the chapel on "E" Street was remodeled, adding over 3,000 square feet of space, and, in November 1997, Evergreen opened the Evergreen's Eagle River Funeral Home in Eagle River, Alaska.

Evergreen Memorial Chapels continues to serve more families than any other funeral home in all of Alaska, providing funeral services, cremation, and casket sales.

❖
The Evergreen Memorial Chapel foyer at 737 "E" Street, Anchorage, Alaska.

ALASKA PERMANENT CAPITAL MANAGEMENT COMPANY

Alaska Permanent Capital Management Company (APCM) is the first major money management firm in Alaska designed to serve Alaska's institutional investors. David and Frances Rose, Alaskans recognized for their accomplishments in public administration, financial management, economic development, and community service, started the company in 1992.

The Roses moved to Alaska in 1960 from New York City. David has a BS in accounting from Queens College and a MBA from Syracuse University. He served on active duty in Alaska with the U.S. Army. Fran has a BA in history from Queens College and a M.Ed. in adult education from the University of Alaska.

David started working in Alaska in 1961 with the U.S. Army as a civilian and was eventually appointed comptroller. In 1975 he was appointed the first executive director of the Alaska Municipal Bond Bank, in 1979 he served as the first executive director of the Alaska Industrial Development Authority, and in 1982 was appointed the first executive director for the Alaska Permanent Fund Corporation. During his tenure at the fund it grew from $3.8 billion to $13.5 billion. He served with local government for ten years and was the first chairman of the Unified Anchorage Municipal Assembly. In addition to being chairman of APCM, David currently serves as vice-chair of the Alaska Pacific University Foundation, has served as co-chair

of the Anchorage Concert Association Endowment Campaign and raises funds for the American Diabetes Association.

Fran taught Adult Basic Education at the Anchorage Community College for thirteen years, six of which she served as the program's director. In 1980 she became city administrator for the City of Akutan. Following the family's move to Juneau, she served in state government in many capacities. She later owned and operated a clothing store called "Victoria's" in Juneau. In addition to her current position as Senior Vice President for Administration at APCM, she is managing partner of Downtown Investments Company, Downtown Deli, Inc., and is on the board of regents of the University of Alaska.

APCM operates as an independent investment advisor and institutional investment manager to Alaskan clients. It is wholly owned and operated by its Alaska resident employees. APCM exclusively seeks Alaska public and private sector institutional accounts and specializes in providing its clients professional, conservative, low cost, and client tailored services. It manages approximately $1.5 billion.

Although they have many professional accomplishments, the Roses are proudest of their family. They have two sons, Evan Denali, who works at APCM, and Mitchell Franklin, a vice-president of the Disney Corporation. They also have three grandchildren.

✧

Left: David Allan Rose, founder of Alaska Permanent Capital Management Company.

Right: Alaska Permanent Capital Management Company's Senior Vice President Frances H. Rose.
COURTESY OF NELSON PHOTOGRAPHY.

SUPERIOR PLUMBING & HEATING, INC.

No matter how attractive a building is on the exterior, if the interior mechanical system doesn't work, neither does the building. For thirty-five years, Alaskans have turned to Superior Plumbing & Heating, Inc. to make sure their projects succeed.

Marion Fox and Bob Pope founded Superior Plumbing & Heating, Inc. (SPHI) in 1964. In 1978, they hired Jan Van Den Top, now president. "I am a mechanical engineer by training—heating, ventilation, plumbing," Van Den Top said. "They needed a successor and I wanted to put my training into practice. It sounded like the way to do it." Van Den Top found the work challenging. "In a three person operation, you can't specialize in anything. I did a little bit of everything."

Customer service is one reason SPHI has thrived in Alaska's volatile economy while others have not. To provide high quality service,

SPHI has expanded to three divisions—Superior Plumbing & Heating, Alaska Sheet Metal, and the SPHI LINC® Service Division. "We offer the total package," Van Den Top says. "Design, installation, and maintenance." SPHI has come a long way from its humble beginnings. Between the three divisions, SPHI now employs 60 to 110 persons, depending upon the projects underway at any given time.

Having quality control on all aspects of a job gives SPHI the flexibility to work successfully in both urban Anchorage and rural Alaska, so their laundry list of successful projects is colorful and varied. Projects currently underway include the Government Hill School remodeling and expansion in Anchorage and the Kaktovik Power Plant on the North Slope. Past projects include the recently completed air conditioning system in the downtown Anchorage Hilton Hotel, and the mechanical systems at the Alaska Airlines terminal in Bethel, and the Alaska Sea Life Center in Seward. Van Den Top found the Sea Life Center an especially rewarding project. SPHI was responsible for piping for the tanks, the filters and the ozone system. "It was an interesting project," he says. "Very unusual." Other projects include the Alyeska Prince Hotel in Girdwood and the Project '80s addition to the Anchorage Museum of History and Art, where the reflecting pool in the main lobby presented a special challenge.

SPHI's ability to meet the needs of their customers—no matter where the project is located—has placed them consistently among Alaska's top five construction contractors. That kind of success can only come from a team of dedicated professionals—professionals who will make sure SPHI continues to get the job done.

✧

Above: Anchorage Museum Atrium Pool.
COURTESY OF TOM ARNOT.

Below: Alaska Sealife Center filter tanks, Seward, Alaska, 1998.
COURTESY OF TOM ARNOT.

Ron Eagley, owner of Gwennie's Old Alaska Restaurant, believes that everybody in Anchorage has eaten at Gwennie's at least once. He's probably right—Gwennie's Old Alaska Restaurant has been a favorite of Anchorage residents and visitors for thirty-five years.

Gwennie and Ronnie Onstead first opened Gwennie's in 1965. The first restaurant was located in a small building between Benson and Northern Lights Boulevard on Spenard Road. Eventually the building became too small to support the growing business and in 1980 the Onsteads moved the restaurant to its current location, 4333 Spenard Road.

The building into which they moved Gwennie's had already established a reputation in Anchorage, although one of a somewhat dubious nature. Since its construction in 1972, the building was home to a brothel and gambling house, which had been shut down just before the Onsteads purchased it. Gwennie's new home was much larger than its original location, and what started as a small family business soon grew larger than what the Onsteads wanted. They sold the restaurant in 1981 to current owner, Ron Eagley.

Gwennie's currently employs about 60 persons in the busy summer months and 50 in the winter. Although the two-story restaurant can seat two hundred hungry people, there is often a waiting list for a table—especially on Sunday mornings. Visitors and locals alike are fascinated with the restaurant's collection of antiques and photographs. The photographs depict everything in Alaskan history from construction of the railroad in Skagway to the running of the Iditarod. Patrons are greeted at the front door with one of Anchorage's most

thorough collections of photographs of the 1964 Good Friday earthquake, which hang in the bar and waiting area.

Gwennie's is a family restaurant, and the pond on the first floor especially mesmerizes children. People are encouraged to throw coins into it and make a wish. The coins actually do make wishes come true as the proceeds collected from well-wishers are donated to "Wish Upon The Northern Star," an organization that grants wishes to seriously ill children in Alaska.

Gwennie's is a locally owned, long-time Alaskan business that contributes a great deal to the community. Besides its donations to the "Wish Upon The North Star" foundation, it provides pre-game meals for the University of Alaska Anchorage hockey team, and the women's volleyball and basketball teams. It also sponsors Little League baseball and PeeWee Hockey teams, to name just a few.

❖

Above: Gwennie's Old Alaska Restaurant located at 4333 Spenard Road.

Below: A friendly bear guards Gwennie's Old Alaska Restaurant Wishing Well.

ALASKA
MILL & FEED

✧

*Above: Alaska Mill & Feed is located at
1501 East First Avenue in Anchorage.*

*Below: Don Donatello was presented the
"Small Businessman of the Year" award in
1965 by President Lyndon Johnson.*

How "Don" Donatello turned a part-time bleach making business into Anchorage's favorite source for garden supplies and Christmas trees is very much an Alaskan success story. A combination of hard work and a talent for spotting new opportunities has resulted in the development of Alaska Mill and Feed. Donatello was awarded the "Small Businessman of the Year" award in 1965 by President Lyndon B. Johnson, and in 1995 was inducted into the Alaska Business Hall of Fame.

Donatello was born Dominic Donatello in 1918 to Italian immigrants in Boston. He earned a degree in chemical engineering at the Massachusetts Institute of Technology and came to Alaska in 1943 as an aircraft maintenance officer stationed on the Aleutian chain. He met his wife, Jean Landstrom, in 1945 on a boat from Seward to Seattle. Jean was born in Anchorage to parents who had come to Alaska during the gold rush. They were married in 1947.

Don started his business in 1947 by mixing bleach in the basement of their Anchorage home in his spare time. As his cottage industry grew, Don began supplying a wider variety of cleaners to his customers. Donatello was soon so busy that he went into business on his own in 1949. He bought large tanks at Merrill Field, where he operated until residential construction moved into the area. He purchased land at First Avenue and Orca Street, where Alaska Mill & Feed and Alaska Garden & Pet Supply are located today.

In 1958 Don entered the rendering business using meat and bones leftover from butcher shops. This led him into the manufacturing of soap and animal feed. The feed mill was built in 1965, and eventually led into the retail and fertilizer businesses. Alaska Mill & Feed now has fifty-five full-time employees. Today, a customer can pull up to the store at 1501 East First Avenue and buy everything from marigolds to horse feed to rabbits at the same location.

Alaska Mill & Feed is very much a family business. All five of the Don and Jean's children have been involved in the business. Don would like to thank his wife for her unending help, his brother George J. Donatello for his assistance, and his children—George C. Donatello, Ben Donatello, Mary Hines, Liz Sherwood, and Margaret Donatello. Donatello is also very appreciative of Ken Sherwood, who has taken over the current operation of the business. He especially wants to thank the many hard working employees, past and present, who have helped his vision to come to life.

Tryck Nyman Hayes, Inc. (TNH) is an Anchorage-based engineering firm that has helped build Alaska for more than forty-seven years. With a solid reputation and diversity of professional expertise, TNH has invested in meeting the needs of Alaska and the Pacific Rim.

The firm originated in 1953 when Charles W. Tryck joined the firm of Rutledge, Johnson & Associates, which was founded in 1951. Frank Nyman became a partner in 1958 creating Tryck, Nyman & Associates. In 1960 Joe L. Hayes joined them creating Tryck, Nyman & Hayes. When the firm incorporated in 1991, it became Tryck Nyman Hayes, Inc.

Brought together by entrepreneurship and contracting opportunities with the Department of Defense and the growing Alaska economy, the engineering expertise of the owners has been a driving force in the firm's success. Charles Tryck was a civil engineer with expertise in municipal planning, surveys, construction control, and management. Frank Nyman's name is linked with the major water and sewer system designs in Anchorage. Joe Hayes brought experience in street and road design, as well as land and subdivision development. Diversification of the firm has resulted in TNH's new owners joining the firm. Ted Trueblood brings railroad engineering and project management expertise and Michael Shoemaker's experience is in marine engineering and Department of Defense communication facilities.

In the past thirty years, TNH has grown from its small beginnings to a firm with more than sixty professional and technical personnel with revenues that exceeded $7 million in 2000. TNH provides engineering, surveying, landscape architecture, and planning services for both private and public clients throughout the world.

Past projects have included the Anchorage Ship Creek water treatment plant and the largest sewage and wastewater treatment system in Alaska; upgrading the East/West runway and design of the North/South runway at the Ted Stevens International Airport; the Point Campbell/Kincaid Park Master Plan, the largest municipal park in Anchorage; location of the one-hundred-mile natural gas pipeline from Beluga to Anchorage; and the 2,100-foot long and 60-foot high C Street Viaduct, linking Anchorage with Government Hill. Current projects include the Alaska Railroad Passenger Depot at the Ted Stevens International Airport and the Port of Anchorage Intermodal Marine Facility, which will link the tourism industry with Alaska; the Alaska Railroad track realignments from Anchorage to the Mat-Su Valley, improving the quality of life for Anchorage commuters and travelers; and the national award-winning Earthquake Park Interpretative Facility.

✧

Bottom, left: TNH's Anchorage headquarters.

Bottom, right: TNH founders Charles Tryck (left), Frank Nyman (center), and Joe Hayes.

AeroTech Flight Service

Richard and Ramona Ardaiz drove into Anchorage from California in 1952. Richard loved aviation and he had heard that Alaska needed pilots. He was right—within a day, he landed a job with Northern Consolidated Airlines (later Wien Air Alaska). Four years later they started what is now one of Alaska's best-known and most prestigious flight schools—AeroTech Flight Service, Inc.

When the Ardaiz's arrived with their two-year-old son, they were "flat broke." The only hotel room they could find in Anchorage was at the Palace Hotel for $27 a night, a third of their entire savings. In the morning Richard announced he was going to look for a job. Unbeknownst to them, Anchorage was experiencing a serious housing shortage. A look through the *Anchorage Times* revealed few choices. They found a house on Sixth Avenue that was way too much money and a tarpaper cabin for $65 a month. They took the cabin. They also used their "California car" (radio, no heater) during their first winter until they could afford one with a heater in January.

In 1956 Richard convinced Ramona they should open a flight school. "He didn't think I had enough to do," she laughs. Their first office was in an old shack on 5th Avenue. In February they leased a Piper Cub from the local Piper Dealer and hired a flight instructor. By July they had purchased two 75 horsepower planes with radios and in 1958 added a Cessna 150. Demand for pilots and training increased so that AeroTech needed larger office space. They moved to their current location, 1100 Merrill Field Drive, in 1968. By then they had trained about 4,000 pilots. AeroTech now has nine airplanes and Ramona has lost count of the number of students they've trained. AeroTech also provides flightseeing services.

Ramona has been referred to as Alaska's "Mother Hen" of aviation. In 1998 the National Avionics Board presented her with the Katherine Wright Memorial Award honoring outstanding women in aviation. When the announcement came in the mail, she assumed it was a mistake because—unlike her husband—she is not a pilot. "That's my husband's thing," she says. But the award, named after Wilbur and Orville Wright's sister, was indeed meant for her. The award is quite prestigious; other winners include Mrs. Lear, Mrs. Cessna, and Mrs. Piper.

Richard and Ramona have been married fifty-three years, and have five children and eight grandchildren. "It has been a lot of fun," Ramona says. "A lot of work, but lots of fun."

INDEX

SPONSORS

ABOUT THE AUTHOR

JOHN STROHMEYER

John Strohmeyer, a Pulitzer Prize-winning journalist and critically acclaimed author, has lived in Alaska since 1987. He has nearly sixty years of professional writing experience and has taught at prestigious universities across the country, including Lehigh University and Penn State before joining the Alaska university system.

In 1972, while editor of the *Bethlehem Globe-Times* in Pennsylvania, Strohmeyer won the Pulitzer Prize for editorial writing. He has been picked as a Pulitzer Prize juror on five different occasions and has served on the boards of the American Society of Newspaper Editors and the Pennsylvania Society of Newspaper Editors, which he headed as president. After leaving the life of daily deadlines, Strohmeyer wrote *Crisis in Bethlehem*, which reviewers described as a classic account of Big Steel's battle to survive.

Strohmeyer came to Alaska in 1987 upon winning appointment as Atwood Professor of Journalism, an endowed chair at the University of Alaska Anchorage. After his term expired, he spent the next years researching the impact of the discovery of oil upon Alaska. His book *Extreme Conditions: Big Oil and the Transformation of Alaska*, published by Simon & Schuster, was nationally acclaimed.

As writer-in-residence at the University of Alaska Anchorage, he continues to research and write about issues generated by what he calls "this fast-changing but still majestic last frontier."